Women of the
American Revolution

Other Books in the History Makers Series:

*History*MAKERS

Women of the
American Revolution

By Mary R. Furbee

Lucent Books
P.O. Box 289011, San Diego, CA 92198-9011

Library of Congress Cataloging-in-Publication Data

Furbee, Mary R. (Mary Rodd), 1954–
    Women of the American Revolution / by Mary R. Furbee.
        p.   cm. — (History makers)
    Includes bibliographical references and index.
    Summary: Discusses the contributions of various women who
helped the American colonies break free of British rule, including
Abigail Adams, Peggy Arnold, Esther Reed, Deborah Sampson,
Mercy Warren, and Phillis Wheatley.
    ISBN 1-56006-489-7 (lib. bdg. : alk. paper)
    1. United States—History—Revolution, 1775–1783—Women—
Juvenile literature.   2. United States—History—Revolution, 1775–1783
—Biography—Juvenile literature.   3. Women—United States—
Biography—Juvenile literature.   [1. United States—History—
Revolution, 1775–1783—Women.   2. Women—Biography.]   I. Title.
II. Series.
E276.F87   1999
973.3'082—dc21   98-53041
                                                                            CIP
                                                                            AC

Printed in the U.S.A.

CONTENTS

The literary form most often referred to as "multiple biography" was perfected in the first century A.D. by Plutarch, a perceptive and talented moralist and historian who hailed from the small town of Chaeronea in central Greece. His most famous work, *Parallel Lives*, consists of a long series of biographies of noteworthy ancient Greek and Roman statesmen and military leaders. Frequently, Plutarch compares a famous Greek to a famous Roman, pointing out similarities in personality and achievements. These expertly constructed and very readable tracts provided later historians and others, including playwrights like Shakespeare, with priceless information about prominent ancient personages and also inspired new generations of writers to tackle the multiple biography genre.

The Lucent History Makers series proudly carries on the venerable tradition handed down from Plutarch. Each volume in the series consists of a set of six to eight biographies of important and influential historical figures who were linked together by a common factor. In *Rulers of Ancient Rome*, for example, all the figures were generals, consuls, or emperors of either the Roman Republic or Empire; while the subjects of *Fighters Against American Slavery*, though they lived in different places and times, all shared the same goal, namely the eradication of human servitude. Mindful that politicians and military leaders are not (and never have been) the only people who shape the course of history, the editors of the series have also included representatives from a wide range of endeavors, including scientists, artists, writers, philosophers, religious leaders, and sports figures.

Each book is intended to give a range of figures—some well known, others less known; some who made a great impact on history, others who made only a small impact. For instance, by making Columbus's initial voyage possible, Spain's Queen Isabella I, featured in *Women Leaders of Nations*, helped to open up the New World to exploration and exploitation by the European powers. Unarguably, therefore, she made a major contribution to a series of events that had momentous consequences for the entire world. By contrast, Catherine II, the eighteenth-century Russian queen, and Golda Meir, the modern Israeli prime minister, did not play roles of global impact; however, their policies and actions significantly influenced the historical development of both their own countries and their regional neighbors. Regardless of their relative importance in the greater historical scheme, all of the figures chronicled in the History Makers series made contributions to posterity; and their public achievements, as well as what is known about their private lives, are presented and evaluated in light of the most recent scholarship.

In addition, each volume in the series is documented and substantiated by a wide array of primary and secondary source quotations. The primary source quotes enliven the text by presenting eyewitness views of the times and culture in which each history maker lived; while the secondary source quotes, taken from the works of respected modern scholars, offer expert elaboration and/ or critical commentary. Each quote is footnoted, demonstrating to the reader exactly where biographers find their information. The footnotes also provide the reader with the means of conducting additional research. Finally, to further guide and illuminate readers, each volume in the series features photographs, two bibliographies, and a comprehensive index.

The History Makers series provides both students engaged in research and more casual readers with informative, enlightening, and entertaining overviews of individuals from a variety of circumstances, professions, and backgrounds. No doubt all of them, whether loved or hated, benevolent or cruel, constructive or destructive, will remain endlessly fascinating to each new generation seeking to identify the forces that shaped their world.

Daughters of Liberty

During the American Revolution, women sewed flags, tore sheets into bandages, and threw flowers at the feet of General George Washington. At home, women boycotted British goods, sewed uniforms, and raised funds for the Continental army. On the front lines, women spied and nursed the wounded. In Philadelphia, New York, and Boston, they published newspapers and rallied in the streets. On the frontier, armed with pitchforks and shovels, they helped defend cabins and forts. All over the thirteen colonies, they grieved over fallen brothers, fathers, sons, and husbands.

The women of the American Revolution were not generals or presidents, for women were excluded from public positions in colonial times. Only men voted in elections and held public offices. Men also controlled the colonial households. For example, husbands took care of family finances, made the rules, and decided how the children would be raised. Wives, meanwhile, ran the households' day-to-day activities. Life was equally segregated for children: Boys helped their fathers, and girls helped their mothers.

The Many Roles of Women

Yet despite women's private and domestic roles, by the end of the war many were "reading widely in political literature, publishing their own sentiments, engaging in heated debates over public policy and avidly supporting the war effort in a variety of ways,"[1] historian Mary Beth Norton writes. Abigail Adams, Mercy Warren, Peggy Arnold, and Esther Reed were among them. All four were reared in prominent families of mostly English ancestry, and all received at least a basic education. Because these women left letters and diaries—and grew up to marry colonial leaders—we know a good bit about their lives. During the Revolution, while their husbands waged war, they managed their family plantations, businesses, and households alone. Three lent their talents to the patriot, or "rebel," cause, while one sided with the British.

Abigail Adams and Mercy Warren were intellectuals and very political. Abigail, very much ahead of her time, debated ideas about women's rights with top leaders of the day. She wrote hun-

During the American Revolution, women sewed flags and uniforms, made bandages, and raised funds for the Continental army.

dreds of letters to Revolutionary leaders, including her Continental congressman husband, John Adams. Later those letters were published and did much to influence new generations of equal rights advocates. Mercy was a prolific letter writer, too. But she also wrote for publication. While her husband got involved in political activities, Mercy wrote popular patriotic plays and poems that ridiculed the British. Because it wasn't acceptable for a woman to be a writer, she wrote anonymously.

Esther Reed and Peggy Arnold also were married to colonial movers and shakers. However, they were focused more on action than ideas. Both hatched schemes to accomplish ambitious goals. Esther, an Englishwoman who recently arrived in the colonies, organized a women's relief organization that raised money for the struggling rebel army. Peggy worked side by side with her husband, the famous traitor Benedict Arnold, to betray the Americans.

Women of less prominent classes and of minority groups also played critical roles in the Revolution. Many people are surprised to learn how many colonial women worked outside the home. Along with raising large families, women worked as farmers, shopkeepers, boardinghouse owners, newspaper publishers, midwives, bakers, and millers. Women turned their homes into hospitals and organized boycotts. Although less is known about their contributions—in part because women who were not educated left

Women rallied together to play a critical role in the Revolution—turning their homes into hospitals and organizing boycotts of British goods.

fewer written documents—servants, slaves, and Native American women also played important roles in the struggle. For example, Native clan mothers—female tribal leaders—influenced whether their tribes allied themselves with the British or the Americans.

Deborah Sampson and Phillis Wheatley were two extraordinary "ordinary" women. Deborah's courage proved that women could be more than "frail flowers." Unhappy with her life as a Massachusetts servant girl, Deborah disguised herself as a man and served as a Continental soldier. By walking her own path, she helped change society's ideas about what women could endure and accomplish. Phillis did the same. A religious Boston family bought the seven-year-old house slave and gave her an education. In a short time, she was more learned than most privileged white girls. Her talents led her to become a celebrated poet, whose accomplishments challenged commonly held views about black and female inferiority.

Ideals of Freedom and Equality

The women in this book were different in many ways. But they also had much in common. All were spirited, talented, well read—and determined to be involved in the struggles of their time. The struggle for freedom inspired them to fight, write, spy, and organize—things females didn't normally do. Because all hands were needed, society began to accept the idea of women adopting new, less domestic, roles. In hundreds of letters and documents, George

Washington, John Adams, Thomas Jefferson, and other founding fathers sang the praises of the "Daughters of Liberty."

That did not, however, mean that male leaders believed women in general were equal to men. Before the war, British law said that men ruled governments and the home, and women did not have the right to vote or own property. After the Revolution, American law said the same. For farsighted women, this was hard to accept. But America was not yet ready to apply the principles of democracy, liberty, and equality to people of both sexes and all races.

Ideals of freedom and equality, however, are hard to contain once they are spoken. Norton writes,

> The change in women's political perceptions wrought by revolutionary circumstances was truly momentous. For the first time, women became active—if not equal—participants in the discourse on public affairs and in endeavors that carried political significance.[2]

After the Revolution, change continued to take place in America. For example, more people taught their daughters to be independent. Public and private schools for girls and young women also opened, and new generations educated in those schools grew ever more committed to principles of equal rights for all. It would take 125 long years after the Revolution for American women to win the right to vote. But the seeds of liberty had been sown long before by the pioneering women of the American Revolution.

CHAPTER 1

The Seeds of Rebellion

American colonists were independent thinkers long before the first shots of the Revolution were fired. For a hundred years, European men and women had come to Britain's thirteen American colonies seeking adventure, wealth, land, and religious or political freedom. The settlers carved farms, plantations, and towns out of dense wilderness. In 1700, 200,000 people had arrived; seventy-five years later, there were 2 million. Colonists saw themselves as British subjects but gradually became more self-reliant.

A Land of Opportunity

European settlers came to the colonies in search of land to call their own—something they could never hope to have in their homelands. Land speculators grew wealthy buying, surveying, and selling land. Younger sons of gentry, who could not inherit land in Europe, also came and prospered. They bought large plantations and began growing and exporting tobacco, indigo (blue dye), wheat, cattle, and rum. Planters also imported African slaves. For the slaves, America was not a land of opportunity but a prison.

Penniless indentured servants and militia soldiers, however, fared better than slaves. With no cash to offer for land, they worked or served in the militia for four to seven years. In exchange, they were given fifty acres to call their own. Many colonists also risked the ever-present wrath of hostile Indians to settle remote and rugged wilderness land on the frontier. In America, land ownership gave white men the right to vote and put poor families on the path to comfort and respectability.

North America was such a land of golden opportunity, in fact, that great European powers battled again and again over which empire would control it.

Empires Battle for Control

In the 1760s, British redcoats and colonial soldiers had just won one nine-year struggle for control of the New World: the French and Indian War. Although primarily a struggle between France

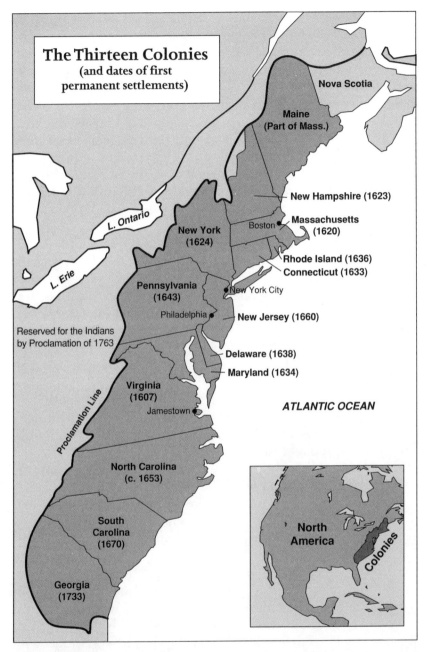

The Thirteen Colonies
(and dates of first
permanent settlements)

Nova Scotia

Maine
(Part of Mass.)

New Hampshire (1623)

Massachusetts
(1620)

Boston

New York
(1624)

Rhode Island (1636)
Connecticut (1633)

L. Ontario

L. Erie

Pennsylvania
(1643)

New York City

Philadelphia

New Jersey (1660)

Reserved for the Indians
by Proclamation of 1763

Delaware (1638)

Maryland (1634)

Virginia
(1607)

ATLANTIC OCEAN

Jamestown

Proclamation Line

North Carolina
(c. 1653)

South
Carolina
(1670)

North
America

Colonies

Georgia
(1733)

and England, the war got its name because most Native American tribes sided with the French in that conflict. The tribes hoped to stop the swarm of land-hungry British subjects from taking more Indian lands.

Colonists rejoiced when the French were driven back across the Atlantic Ocean—and the Indians had retreated west of the

Appalachian Mountains. But the rejoicing was soon replaced by anger toward the mother country, Britain.

After fighting alongside redcoats to defeat the French, the land-hungry colonists thought it was time to defeat the Indians once and for all. They wanted to pursue the Indians, defeat them, and claim the western lands as their own. But King George III of England shocked them by saying no. Britain had borrowed a great deal of money to pay for the war, and the king wanted no more expense. He forbade colonists to attack the Indians or move onto their lands. Then, to make matters worse, the British Parliament decided that American colonists should pay Britain's war debts.

A Taxing Trouble

To pay war debts from the French and Indian War, British Parliament passed the Sugar, Stamp, and Townshend Acts during the 1760s and early 1770s. These English laws forced colonists to pay taxes on molasses, newspapers, books, playing cards, glass, tea, and other goods shipped to the colonies. Before King George's ascension to the throne in 1760, Parliament had mostly left the colonists alone to govern themselves. And colonists had been too independent for too long to accept these taxes. Yet that is not all that upset them.

White American colonists considered themselves English subjects who deserved to be represented in Parliament. Without a vote, many colonists felt they were "no better than slaves." Others, however, thought these democratic ideas were nonsense and Parliament had the right to rule and tax the colonies as it saw fit.

Soon men and women in all thirteen of the American colonies had joined the debate. And they were far from united. About half the colonists supported the rebels; one-quarter stayed loyal to Britain; and one-quarter tried to stay neutral. Among the "loyalists" were several thousand blacks who escaped slavery and joined the British. Some of these slaves were granted their freedom by the British and relocated to Canada or England after the war. But many were resold into slavery. White colonists who stayed loyal to Britain had various reasons. Some took seriously their sworn allegiance to the English king. Others depended on trade with Britain. Many members of the religious Quakers and Shaker groups initially opposed the pro-independence revolutionaries, who they considered far too rash and rebellious. Members of these religions were also opposed to violence and warfare. After the fighting broke out, Shakers remained fiercely opposed to war, and some leaders were jailed for publicly preaching against it. Quak-

14

ers, however, split over which side to support. Many avoided the conflict altogether. Some collaborated with the British or the patriots but would not take up arms. Still others abandoned their pacifism and joined the British or American army.

Loyalists and rebels debated British policies and taxes in taverns, parlors, newspapers, and the streets. To oppose the new taxes, many colonists started refusing to buy British goods. Rebel women made their own tea from raspberry leaves and paper from tree bark; they also held public spinning bees to make homespun cloth. Secret organizations—the Sons of Liberty and the Daughters of Liberty—organized rallies in the streets. The crowds forced royal customs agents, men who collected the British taxes, to resign. Then, in Boston, the protests turned bloody.

Protest Turns to Revolt

On March 5, 1770, a group of Boston men and women held a demonstration against British taxes. The crowd threatened a customs office guard, and British soldiers arrived to protect him. The colonists threw snowballs, then rocks. The British soldiers responded by firing into the crowd, killing five colonists.

Many women protested the collection of British taxes by refusing to buy British goods, making their own cloth and tea, organizing rallies, or forcing customs agents to resign.

The tragic Boston Massacre shocked even the British. To keep the peace, Parliament canceled all the taxes except the one on tea. Much of the popular fury toward Britain died down—but not all of it. A small group of radical colonists were upset about a new law, the Declaratory Act, which said that Parliament had an absolute right to make laws governing its colonies. To most colonists, the five dead men of Boston were the tragic victims of a riot that successfully caused the British to back down. But to the radicals, the riot was evidence of British tyranny—and the dead men were the first martyrs in the coming showdown over independence.

For three years, the radicals blew on the embers of anti-British feelings until they again burst into flames. Influential rebel thinkers and writers—Patrick Henry, Phillis Wheatley, Mercy Warren, Thomas Paine, and others—churned out plays, poems, pamphlets, and articles ridiculing the British. But it took a harmless brown plant—tea—to set off the powder keg of war.

Before 1773, colonial tea merchants had bought crates of tea from the British and resold it to local shopkeepers. Then the British started selling the tea directly to the colonial shopkeepers. The tea middlemen were put out of business by this new bit of "British treachery." So they joined forces with the radicals in working for independence.

On December 16, 1773, three British ships filled with tea sat in Boston Harbor. The radicals and merchants, disguised as Indians,

Radicals dressed as Indians dump British tea into the harbor. This event, known as the Boston Tea Party, sparked the war for independence.

boarded the ship and dumped the tea into the harbor. The raiders knew the British would punish colonists for dumping the tea. The men also knew that many colonists would resent that punishment and join the fight for independence. And that's just what happened.

The Die Is Cast

After the Boston Tea Party, the British closed the port of Boston and banned town meetings. Then they shipped thousands of British soldiers to the colonies and forced colonists to house and feed them. Many colonial women quartering redcoats took the opportunity to listen in on the officers' conversations—and report what they heard to rebel leaders. Women also resumed their boycott. In Edenton, North Carolina, fifty-one women signed and published a paper pledging to boycott all British goods and telling other women they had a "duty" to do the same.

It wasn't long before protest turned to rebellion. In Philadelphia on September 5, 1774, colonial representatives formed the First Continental Congress. It stated that colonists had a right to set their own taxes and make their own laws. Congress also decided to collect military supplies and form armies.

Forced to quarter British troops, women signed and published a pledge to boycott all British goods.

Still, many colonists hoped to avoid war. A group of loyalist Quakers wrote to King George III and begged him to make changes. But King George III wrote back, "The die is now cast, the Colonies must either submit or triumph." [3]

In April 1775, the two sides clashed on battlefields in Lexington, Massachusetts, and Concord, New Hampshire, forcing the British troops back to Boston. Soon after, the Second Continental Congress met in Philadelphia and formally declared war on Britain. The Congress appointed Colonel George Washington of Virginia as commander in chief of the American forces. Then on July 4, 1776, the Declaration of Independence was adopted. In July, a huge British force arrived in New York Harbor, ready to crush the rebellion.

On the Battlefield

The Americans lost many battles in the year after independence was declared. The British bombarded South Carolina and for months at a time occupied Trenton, Princeton, Boston, New York, and Philadelphia. Washington endured the bitterly cold winter of 1776–1777 at Valley Forge, without enough food, clothing, and supplies. Then, in October 1777, the tide turned when the Continental army defeated the British at Saratoga, New York.

The patriots were a determined bunch, but the victory at Saratoga didn't change one fact: Britain had many more soldiers, ships, and guns. America needed help, and France gave it. On February 6, 1778, at the urging of Benjamin Franklin, France signed a treaty of alliance with America.

In 1778, the British captured the major southern ports of Savannah, Georgia, and Charleston, South Carolina. But the allied French and American navies also won several battles. In 1780, Peggy Arnold joined her husband in a traitorous (but foiled) plot to hand rebel-held West Point over to the British. Also in 1781, Esther Reed founded a women's association that collected funds and supplies for the Continental army. By October 19, 1781, at Yorktown near the mouth of Chesapeake Bay, British general Cornwallis's army of eight thousand British soldiers surrendered.

Despite the surrender, the war dragged on for two more years—leaving plenty of opportunity for Private Robert Shurtleff (Deborah Sampson Gannett) to engage some redcoats in battle. Peace negotiations, however, had begun. On September 3, 1783, the warring sides signed the Treaty of Paris, creating a free and independent nation: the United States of America.

CHAPTER 2

Abigail Smith Adams (1744–1818)

Abigail Adams never won a battle, held an important post, or wrote for publication. As historian Elizabeth Evans notes, only private words in private letters earned her a place in history as "America's most famous advocate of women's rights."[4] Ideas about liberty swept through the population and led Abigail to challenge commonly held ideas. In letters written to her Continental congressman husband John Adams, as well as other leaders, Abigail voiced her Revolutionary views. In 1776, she coined a phrase that became a rallying cry for later generations that fought for women's equality: "Remember the Ladies."[5]

Historian Rosemary Keller writes, "Certain persons stand out as early witnesses to the possibility of a new way of life and self-understanding. Abigail Adams is one of them. She extended the meaning of the Declaration of Independence to women and acted on its principles in her daily life."[6]

"Wild Colts Make Good Horses"

Abigail Smith was born on November 11, 1744. Her father, William Smith, was a Congregationalist minister. Her mother, Elizabeth Quincy Smith, traced her ancestors to New England's first settlers. William and Elizabeth lived in the peaceful village of Weymouth, Massachusetts, and had four children: Abigail, her sisters Mary and Betsy, and one brother, William. The family was comfortably well to do, but not

Through her revolutionary ideas, Abigail Adams became known as an advocate of women's rights.

among the colonies' most wealthy. A handful of servants worked in their rambling house, which sat on a hill overlooking a large farm. Numerous relatives, including her merry and supportive Grandmother Quincy, lived nearby and visited often.

Abigail was a serious, happy, and somewhat stubborn child. Often, she was sick, which made her worried mother overprotective. Abigail sometimes complained about her mother's fretting and longed to have more freedom. But occasional stubbornness was her only rebellion, for her parents were loving and she wanted to please them.

Along with her mother's hovering, Abigail had only one other complaint about her childhood—that she did not receive a formal education. When Abigail was a child, her mother taught her and her sisters enough reading, writing, and basic math so that they could read their Bible, pay bills, and write letters. Like most mothers, Elizabeth taught her daughters at home, although a few New England towns did have "dame schools" for girls. In contrast, Abigail's only brother, William, studied history, literature, mathematics, Greek, and Latin. William's teacher was his Harvard-educated father.

Abigail, however, did not let her lack of formal education deter her. Whenever possible, she escaped to the family's extensive library to read her brother's and father's books. Abigail later wrote that even as a child her goal had been to "grow daily in virtue and learning."[7] Abigail's mother, who thought such academic interests "unwomanly," was worried. However, Grandmother Quincy told the family not to worry because "wild colts make good horses."[8] Abigail's father, who loved learning above all else, also supported Abigail's interest in academics. As long as it did not cut into Abigail's other lessons or household duties, he allowed Abigail to read to her heart's content.

Courtship

Many girls feared becoming too educated because some young men criticized clever women as too "masculine." When he first met Abigail Smith, John Adams seemed not to like her for just that reason. The two met at her sister Mary's wedding, when Abigail was fifteen and John was a twenty-seven-year-old lawyer. The Smith girls were "wits," John wrote in his diary. But they were reserved, serious, and not "fond" or gay enough for his liking. By the time Abigail was seventeen, however, John had changed his mind. Now the short, round John found Abigail's intense wide-set eyes appealing—and her serious manner, modest and sensible. Abigail returned John's affection, and fifty years after their marriage she still spoke of being thrilled the first time she held John's hand.

"Dear Partner"

In 1764, twenty-year-old Abigail Smith married John Adams. They moved to a farm in the small seaside village of Braintree, Massachusetts. There the husband she called her "dear partner" began building a country law practice. In four years, the couple had a daughter, then a son. But the peaceful years were not to last.

In Spring 1768, the family moved to Boston, where there were more opportunities for an ambitious young lawyer. The city of sixteen thousand residents was a hotbed of anti-British activity in the American colonies. Although the family had a couple of servants to help with the housework and child rearing, Abigail had her hands full. Washing, cooking, and sewing were backbreaking and time-consuming tasks in an era before electricity and indoor plumbing. Abigail, like most women, also had children in quick succession.

John Adams defended the British soldiers involved in the Boston Massacre.

While in Boston, she gave birth to three more children, one of whom died at eighteen months old. (Infant mortality was high, in part because antibiotics had not been invented to treat infectious diseases.) Yet despite her demanding domestic duties, Abigail found time to read the newspaper daily and discuss politics with John.

Three months after the family came to Boston, in October 1768, seven hundred British artillerymen debarked from ships of war and marched into town, with muskets charged, bayonets fixed, colors flying, drums beating, and fifes playing. Protests stemming from the Stamp Act of 1765 and the Townshend Act of 1767 had inspired Parliament to send the soldiers. The British soldiers were meant to send a strong message. Colonists who did not obey—or protested—the king's laws would be arrested as traitors. Bostonians were deeply resentful of the soldiers' presence, especially since the Quartering Act required citizens to house and feed the soldiers in their homes.

At first, Abigail hoped bloodshed could be avoided. But on March 5, 1770, that hope was shattered. That day, hundreds of men and boys armed with sticks and clubs dashed through the snow-covered street shouting anti-British slogans. The mob swelled to thousands and cornered several British guards at the Boston Customs (tax collection) House and began throwing icicles, rocks, and snowballs at the soldiers. Believing the soldiers would never dare fire their rifles, they taunted: "Fire, damn you, fire! Fire! Fire! Fire!"[9] After awhile, against orders, the soldiers did just that. When the smoke cleared, five American colonists lay dead in the snow.

More radical Sons of Liberty believed the Boston Massacre had been a beneficial development. They believed it would help them rally popular support for their cause. In newspaper articles, pamphlets, and broadsides, they called the British soldiers murderers—and the dead protesters martyrs. Broadsides were widely read flyers plastered all over walls and storefronts in American cities. One read, in part,

AMERICANS!
Bear in Remembrance
THE HORRID MASSACRE!
Perpetrated in King Street, Boston,
New England,
On the Evening of March the Fifth, 1770,
When FIVE of your fellow countrymen,
GRAY, MAVERICK, CALDWELL, ATTUCKS,
and CARR,
Lay wallowing in their GORE!
Being basely, and most inhumanely,
MURDERED! . . .
Forever may America be preserved,
From weak and wicked monarchs,
Tyrannical Ministers,
Abandoned Governors,
Their Underlings and Hirelings!
And may the
Machinations of artful, designing wretches,
Who would ENSLAVE THIS People,
Come to an end. . . .[10]

The radicals' efforts to muster support worked. A quarter to a half of the population of Boston attended the massacre victims' funerals, turning them into huge protest marches. For John and Abigail, however, the massacre created problems. After the British officers were arrested, their friends called on John Adams and asked him to be the prisoners' defense attorney. The men knew John sided with the Sons of Liberty, but they also knew of his strong belief that all men deserved a strong defense and fair trial.

John agreed to defend the soldiers, but it was a frightening decision for the family. By agitating against the Crown, he had been risking arrest by royal officials, as well as confiscation of his family's property. Now, for defending the British sentries, he risked being branded a traitor by fellow rebels. Abigail was worried, but she supported her husband's decision. John wrote,

> That excellent Lady, who has always encouraged me, burst into a flood of Tears, but said she was very sensible of all the danger to her and to our Children as well as to me, but she thought I had done as I ought, she was very willing to share in all that was to come and place her trust in Providence.[11]

In the end, the court found the British soldiers innocent of murder, and the fervor died down. John Adams not only retained the support of key rebel leaders but also won a seat on the Massachusetts Assembly.

More riots and protests followed the Boston Massacre, the most critical of which was the Boston Tea Party on December 16, 1773.

British guards, cornered by an angry mob, shoot five colonists. This event became known as the Boston Massacre.

Abigail strongly approved of the protesters who dumped hundreds of barrels of "baneful weed" into the harbor. "The flame is kindled and like Lightning it catches from Soul to Soul," [12] she wrote to her friend Mercy Warren. The British Parliament, however, wanted to throw water on that spreading flame. "Boston should be punished," one member of Parliament told his colleagues. "She is your eldest son!" [13]

Parliament levied its first punishment on March 31, 1774; the Port Act closed Boston Harbor to all trade. Then King George sent thousands more soldiers, named a Governor's Council to replace the Massachusetts Assembly, and outlawed town meetings. Anger over these heavy-handed laws strengthened public opposition to Britain and Abigail's own convictions. On June 17, John was elected to serve as one of five Massachusetts delegates in the First Continental Congress. He departed for Philadelphia on August 10, and there he would remain for the next three years. On August 19, an excited Abigail wrote,

> I long impatiently to have you upon the Stage of action. The first of the month of September, perhaps may be of as much importance to Great Britain as the Ides of March were to Caesar. I wish you every Publick as well, as private blessing, that wisdom which is profitable both for instruction and edification to conduct you in this difficult day. [14]

To escape the British occupation of Boston, Abigail fled with her children and servants to Braintree. She remained there for most of the war. Even in the country, however, the presence of four thousand redcoats kept residents "in continual expectation of alarms." The closed port also resulted in severe shortages of food and fuel. As she would throughout the war, Abigail wrote detailed letters about conditions in and around Boston. To noted English author and historian Catharine Macaulay, she wrote in October 1774:

> We are invaded with fleets and armies, our commerce not only obstructed but totally ruined, the courts of justice shut, many driven out from the metropolis, thousands reduced to want or dependent upon the charity of their neighbors for a daily supply of food—all the horrors of civil war threatening us on one hand and the chains of slavery ready forged for us on the other. [15]

After the battles of Lexington and Concord on April 19, 1775, the Second Continental Congress met again in Philadelphia. On May 25, two months later, a trio of British generals arrived deter-

A thousand men died in the bloody Battle of Bunker Hill.

mined to put down the rebellion: William Howe, Sir Henry Clinton, and John Burgoyne. On June 15, Congress established a Continental army. On June 17, 1775, the rapid developments of that spring produced the bloody Battle of Bunker and Breed's Hill. From a hilltop on their Braintree farm, Abigail saw her first and only battle being fought. In the distance, thousands of New England minutemen—militia soldiers ready in a minute to fight—tried and failed to evict Britain from Boston. The British sent the rebels packing, although at a heavy cost. A thousand British and four hundred American soldiers were injured or dead.

After the battle, Abigail learned that the family physician and good friend Dr. Warren had been killed in battle. This personal loss—the first of many she would experience throughout the war—inspired one of her most moving letters to her husband. In her grief, she spoke of Warren in the present tense—as if he still lived:

> Not all the havoc and devastation they [the British] have made has wounded me like the death of Warren. We want him in the Senate; we want him in his profession; we want him in the field. We mourn for the citizen, the senator, the physician and the warrior. When he fell, liberty wept.[16]

However, Dr. Warren's death strengthened rather than weakened Abigail's passion for the rebels' cause. "We possess a spirit that will not be conquered," she wrote to her husband. "If our men are all drawn off and we should be attacked, you would find a race of Amazons in America." [17]

To endure hard times that followed, Amazonian strength was truly needed. John was still in Philadelphia, and Abigail alone was responsible for managing the household and farm. Times were hard in many ways. During a smallpox epidemic, Abigail nursed the entire household and watched her mother and a servant die. Farmhands left in the middle of hay-making season to join the army. Prices rose so high that Abigail could not afford to repair the crumbling ceiling and moldy floor. Unused to coping on her own, Abigail hoped in vain that her husband's public service would be temporary. "I dare not express to you how ardently I long for your return," she wrote with a touch of desperation. "I cannot consent to your tarrying much longer . . . your wife and children are in danger of wanting bread." [18]

"Remember the Ladies"

In May 1776, the British retreated from Boston and headed for New York. With the immediate danger to her family gone, Abigail began to turn her mind to politics. On May 22, an impassioned Abigail wrote to a sympathetic English publisher and friend, Edward Dilly:

> A Spirit that prevails among men of all degrees, all ages and sexes is the Spirit of Liberty. For this they are determined to risk all their property and their lives. . . . Every peasant wears his arms, and flies to them with the uttermost eagerness upon every allarms. . . . This Thought we must now bid a final adieu to Britain, nothing will now appease the Exasperated Americans but the heads of those traitors who have subverted the constitution, for the blood of our Brethren crys to us from the Ground. [19]

John Adams continued to serve in Congress and had emerged as a national leader who sat on many committees. Abigail wrote to him often. She expressed her affection, her support, and her ideas on how a free America should be governed. Women's rights were her primary concern, yet she also addressed the need for women's education and the immorality of slavery. Abigail saw herself as her husband's intellectual and political equal and adviser. Sometimes, when she offered advice or opinions in her letters, she signed them "Sister Delegate."

In early 1776, John Adams was helping Thomas Jefferson write the Declaration of Independence. On March 31, Abigail offered her first suggestions "on Behalf of our Sex." Under English law, married women became one with their husbands and had no legal rights of their own. Abigail felt that women should have the right to own property, sign contracts, transact business, and draft wills. Her primary request was that women's "legal subordination" to their husbands be eliminated. With this in mind, Abigail wrote:

> I long to hear that you have declared independency . . . and by the way, in the new Code of Laws which I suppose it will be necessary for you to make, I desire you would Remember the Ladies, and be more generous and favorable to them than your ancestors. Do not put such unlimited power into the hands of Husbands. Remember all Men would be Tyrants if they could.[20]

Perhaps because her views were so bold, Abigail softened her suggestion with her teasing "threat" to rebel.

> If perticuliar care and attention is not paid to the Ladies we are determined to foment a Rebellion, and will not hold ourselves bound by any Laws in which we have no voice, or Representation. . . . That your Sex are naturally Tyrannical is a Truth so thoroughly established as to admit of no dispute, but such of you as wish to be happy willingly give up the harsh title of Master for the more tender and endearing one of friend.[21]

John Adams had always respected the views of his wife. He often called her a better writer than he, his best adviser, and "an excellent Stateswoman."[22] But this time she was too revolutionary even for the revolutionaries. Like the vast majority of Americans, John agreed with Thomas Jefferson that "The tender breasts of ladies were not formed for political convulsion."[23] On April 14, John responded with astonishment and amusement to his "saucy" wife's recommendations. He felt that white men who owned property had every right to rebel against the ruling elite of Britain. But he believed that women, poor white men, servants, blacks, and Indians were meant to be subservient and obedient. He found it an inconceivable idea—laughable even—that liberty and equality would extend to these populations. A vast majority of patriot leaders shared his views.

> As to your extraordinary Code of Laws, I cannot but laugh. We have been told that our struggle has loosened the bands of Government everywhere. That Children and

Apprentices were disobedient. That schools and Colledges were grown turbulent. That Indians slighted their Guardians. And Negroes grew insolent to their Masters. But your letter was the first Intimation that another Tribe more numerous and powerful than all the rest were grown discontented. . . . Depend upon it, We know better than to repeal our Masculine systems. . . . I hope General Washington, and all our brave Heroes would fight.[24]

The Declaration of Independence did not, in the end, extend liberty or equality to blacks, women, or white men who did not own property. But a May 26 letter her husband wrote to a fellow delegate showed Abigail had influenced his thinking—and caused him to worry. The delegate wanted the new Massachusetts Constitution to allow white men who did not own property to vote. A worried John lobbied his fellow delegate to rethink his position:

Depend upon it, Sir, it is dangerous to open so fruitful a course of controversy . . . to alter the qualifications of voters; there will be no end of it. New Claims will arise; women will demand a vote, lads from twelve to twenty-one will think their rights not enough attended to; and every man who has not a farthing, will demand an equal voice with any other, in all acts of state. It tends to confound and destroy all distinctions, and prostrate all ranks to one common level.[25]

After this exchange of letters, Abigail no longer lobbied her husband to consider women's legal rights. But she did not stop asking for information. On April 5, 1776, Abigail wrote to her husband and asked what was going on in the halls of Congress. "If a form of government is to be established here, what one will be assumed?" she asked. "Will it be left to our Assemblies to choose one? And will not many men have many minds?"[26] A month later, she spoke out against slavery: "It has always appeared a most iniquitous scheme to me to fight ourselves for what we are daily robbing from those who have as good a right to freedom as we have."[27] Abigail also addressed education for women. By reading widely, she had educated herself, although she was embarrassed by her poor spelling. Often, she spoke out against the "trifling, narrow . . . education of the females in this country." She justified her views by saying that learned mothers made good sons. "If we mean to have Heroes, Statesmen, and Philosophers," Abigail wrote to John, "we should have learned women."[28]

In 1778, John's term in Congress was over, but he did not return home as his wife had hoped. Instead, he was named commissioner of France and helped Benjamin Franklin negotiate the critical military alliance between the United States and France. Abigail had been farming halfheartedly and barely making ends meet on her husband's small con-

gressman's salary. When her husband left for France, however, she realized it was up to her to knuckle down and rescue the family finances. She began to manage the farm more carefully and made several successful land deals. "Mrs. Adams Native Genius will Excel us all in Husbandry,"[29] Mercy Warren's husband James wrote to John Adams. In addition, Abigail imported merchandise from Holland and resold it through a network of agents.

A Strong Bond

When the French fleet and American army defeated the British at Yorktown in October 1781, Abigail again hoped her husband would return home. But Congress asked John Adams to help negotiate a peace treaty, and that would take two more long years. Although they did not always agree

In their husbands' absence many women, including Abigail Adams, had to manage the farm and finances, and make successful land deals.

with each other, the bond between John and Abigail was deep and strong. From Braintree, Abigail wrote to John in France: "Hope and fear have been the two ruling passions of . . . my life, and I have been bandied from one to the other like a tennis ball. Life is too short to have the dearest of its enjoyments curtailed. . . . Give me the man I love!" John replied as ardently, "I must go to you or you must come to me. I cannot live in this horrid solitude."[30]

In 1784, Abigail sailed to join her husband in France. It had been nearly ten years since the couple had lived together under the same roof. Awaiting her arrival, John boasted to a friend that his "amiable lady" had earned "good title to the character of heroine."[31]

Wife and Mother of Presidents

Abigail continued to write privately about women's rights during her husband's postwar political career. She also accompanied her husband to five diplomatic posts around the world. In 1789, John Adams was elected vice president of the United States. In 1796 he became the second U.S. president. In 1807 Abigail wrote to Mercy Warren and said they both had seen so many changes that they "stood like statues gaping at what we can neither fathom or comprehend." [32]

According to Linda Kerber, "For many women the Revolution had been a strongly politicizing experience . . . but the newly created republic made little for them (women) as political beings." [33] Both were true for Abigail. She had to content herself with encouraging her husband, friends, sons, and daughters to view the world differently.

At age seventy-four, Abigail Adams died of typhoid fever. She lived to see her oldest son, John Quincy Adams, become a U.S. congressman, but she did not live to see him become the sixth president in 1825. Abigail Adams was the only American woman to be both the wife and the mother of U.S. presidents.

CHAPTER 3

Peggy Shippen Arnold (1760–1802)

In September 1780, Peggy and Benedict Arnold attempted to capture George Washington and turn the important fortress West Point over to the British. Benedict Arnold became the most hated man in America; Peggy Arnold became a forgettable footnote. What that footnote said was based largely on guesswork, and changed over time. Until the 1930s, she was portrayed either as a shallow loyalist or a beautiful, innocent girl who had no idea that her husband was a British spy. No one suggested that Peggy had played any important role.

In the 1930s, the truth emerged. The papers of British commander Sir Henry Clinton were made public. They proved that Peggy Shippen Arnold was "actively engaged in the Arnold conspiracy at every step." In fact, Benedict Arnold's biographer, Willard Sterne Randall, calls Peggy Arnold "the highest paid American spy during the American Revolution." [34]

Peggy Arnold's (pictured with daughter) participation with her husband, as a British spy, was not proven by historians until the 1930s.

"The Worst Sex"

Margaret Shippen, called Peggy, was born on June 11, 1760. Her parents, Edward and Margaret Shippen, were upper-class Philadelphians with considerable wealth and real estate holdings. Edward Shippen wrote to his father that his fourth daughter was "entirely welcome" despite being "the worst sex." [35] The Shippens, who also had one son, lived in a Society Hill mansion on South Fourth Street. Formal gardens and orchards surrounded the luxurious home, which was maintained with the help of several slaves and servants. Edward Shippen held important positions as admiralty judge and recorder of deeds.

Peggy grew up hearing her father, Judge Shippen, express frustration over British laws and taxes. Yet the aristocratic judge was not frustrated enough to favor independence. He found it unthinkable for ordinary people to govern, for that was the job of the benevolent, upper-class elite tied to the mother country. When British laws were unjust, they must be challenged in court, he believed, not protested on the streets or fought over on the battlefield. Growing up, Peggy often heard him talk about his fear that social anarchy and chaos would destroy the colonies. "Poor America!" he wrote to his father during the Stamp Act protests of 1765. "It has seen its best days." [36]

Colonists who did not support separation from Britain had many reasons. Some, like Peggy's father, disapproved of independence because they feared democratic ideas that supported giving ordinary people the power to govern. Others took seriously their sworn allegiance to the king. Many Quakers thought independence could be won only with violence, which they opposed on religious grounds. In addition, many colonists stood to lose a great deal if America won the Revolution. Colonial governors and tax collectors, for example, were appointed and handsomely paid by the British royal family. If America became independent, these officials would lose their jobs. Also, many American colonists had grown rich because the king had deeded them large land grants in America; others hoped to benefit in the same way. The owners of these grants grew wealthy by dividing their land into smaller parcels that they sold to land-hungry Americans.

Staying Neutral

In 1774, Peggy was looking forward to becoming a high-society belle. Her sisters assured her that her China-doll features, petite figure, and flirtatious charm would win her many handsome, wealthy—and marriageable—suitors. At age fourteen, Peggy's days were filled with lessons in how to speak French, sing ballads, dance the minuet, and converse with gentlemen callers. The next year, at age fifteen, Peggy expected to make her debut in Philadelphia's social season. Her expectations were dashed, however, thanks to the conflict with Britain.

The First Continental Congress came to Philadelphia in September 1774. Only a few blocks from the Shippen mansion, at Carpenter's Hall, Congress met to discuss how the colonies should respond to the British blockade of Boston Harbor. Judge Shippen, still trying to sit on the political fence, tried to maintain friendly relationships with British officials and patriot leaders alike. British general Thomas Gage and a young British officer named John André dined at the Shippens' home one week. Congressmen George Washington of Virginia and Benedict Arnold of Rhode Island dined there the next.

Another way Peggy's father attempted to stay neutral was to resign his position as a royally appointed judge so he wouldn't have to enforce unpopular British laws. Yet this cut the Shippens' income in a time when prices were sky high. To escape both the political pressure to choose sides and the high cost of expensive dresses and lavish dinners for his daughters' amusement, Judge Shippen took his family to live in the suburbs. Peggy missed the excitement of the city and wrote of her horrid exile in the country. The farmhouse kitchen, she wrote with disdain, smelled of stale grease.

"My Fashionable Daughters"

In the country, the Shippen family lived frugally and saved money. But Peggy's father's attempt to avoid political pressures failed. After 1776, the governing bodies of several states began seizing and selling property of those who would not sign oaths of allegiance to the American cause. Officials in New Jersey and Pennsylvania—the family lived in farmhouses in both states during their exile—began pressuring Judge Shippen to sign such oaths. If he did not, the judge risked losing his large real estate holdings, being banished from the state, and being arrested. Because he favored reform over rebellion and compromise over confrontation, Judge Shippen did not support the rebellion. But after stalling as long as he could, he reluctantly signed the oath in 1777.

On September 25, 1777, while the Shippens bided their time in the countryside, the British forced their way through Washington's troops at Brandywine Creek in Pennsylvania. Half the population of Philadelphia fled. Patriots removed bells from church steeples——including the 2,080-pound Liberty Bell from the Pennsylvania Statehouse tower—so the British couldn't melt them into bullets. Congress hastily fled to the frontier towns of Lancaster, then York. Washington's army, after failing to stop the British at Brandywine, retreated to winter at Valley Forge. Soon after the three thousand British soldiers marched festively into town, the Shippens returned to their city home.

Peggy, now seventeen, was thrilled to be back. She and other teenage girls enthusiastically welcomed the British. War seemed

Dances such as a minuet offered young girls a chance for romance with British soldiers.

far away and irrelevant, but the dashing British officers would ensure a lively, elegant social life. In their diaries, girls of prominent families wrote of forgetting "the calamities of war" and finding a "fine field open for a romantic girl to exhibit in." [37] However, Edward Shippen's financial situation had not improved. He still did not have the cash for the fancy dresses, hairstylists, and entertainments his daughters required, and he considered leaving the city again. To his father, the judge wrote: "The style of life my fashionable daughters have introduced into my family, and their dress, will, I fear, before long, oblige me to change the scene." [38] In the end, however, Peggy and her sisters pleaded with him to find a way. Edward Shippen, an obliging father, sold a New Jersey estate to raise the needed cash.

That winter, a British officer Peggy had briefly met three years earlier became a frequent visitor to the Shippens' mansion. Lieutenant John André—a handsome young officer with a flair for poetry, music, and art—would later become the head of a vast network of British spies in America. He sketched a portrait of seventeen-year-old Peggy and gave her a locket that held a ringlet of his hair, which she kept until she died. Although early writers speculated about a romance, the bits and pieces of surviving evidence suggest more of a flirtatious friendship.

The British officers transformed Philadelphia society during that winter of occupation. Hairstyles grew to be two-foot-tall masterpieces that took hairdressers hours to create. Barges strung with lights became floating dance floors. Laughing groups of young people wrapped in rugs flew down snow-covered hills on giant sleds. A British officer stationed in the city wrote, "Great alterations have taken place since I was here last. It is all gaiety . . . every lady and gentleman endeavors to outdo the other in splendor and show." Peggy—considered a great beauty—was a favorite. "All the young men," one observer wrote, "are in love with Peggy." [39]

Not all Philadelphians joined the revels. Some criticized the "shameful scene of dissipation." Such gaiety seemed "insensible" when the land was "so greatly desolated." [40] That desolation was plain to see only several miles away at Valley Forge. Washington's soldiers wrapped their shoeless feet in rags and left bloody tracks in the snow. Terrible storms crashed in the roofs of two thousand hastily built log huts, burying men "like sheep under the snow." The soldiers were "in a wretched condition for the want of clothes, blankets and shoes." [41]

In May 1778, the British withdrew from Philadelphia to New York. About twelve hundred loyalists fled with them, but the Shippens remained. Still hoping to straddle the political fence, they stayed to greet General Benedict Arnold, the new American military governor of Philadelphia. In May 1775, the renowned General Arnold had captured New York's Fort Ticonderoga without firing a shot. Historian Thomas Fleming writes that the Revolution might have failed early without Benedict Arnold's military leadership.

Radical patriots wanted to arrest city residents who had transacted business with the British during the occupation and charge them with collaborating with the enemy. At the very least, the patriots believed high-society families who had wined and dined the

Although twenty years her senior, Benedict Arnold proposed marriage to Peggy Shippen.

British, such as the Shippens, should be shunned. But General Arnold had other ideas. Under his leadership, the society dinners and balls were as showy as ever. Benedict Arnold and his top officers also welcomed with open arms the Philadelphians who had kept company with the British officers, including Peggy. Before long Benedict Arnold was pursuing Peggy Shippen romantically.

Accusations and Resentment

Many American officers and political officials disliked General Arnold, a New Haven, Connecticut, native. Born in 1741, he had grown up poor in Rhode Island. As a young man, he made a fortune as a smuggler. Although fearless in battle, he had a pushy, argumentative manner that antagonized other military leaders. He borrowed heavily, lived extravagantly, and dressed flashily. Aristocratic officers, in particular, thought him "exceedingly fond of dress" and "without breeding." [42] During Benedict Arnold's command of Philadelphia, he became even more disliked. City and state officials accused him of trading with the enemy, using army wagons for personal business, and giving too many residents "passes" that allowed them to travel to British-held territory. Supposedly, those with passes were doing business with civilians or visiting family members. But the patriots believed that many who used the passes were really giving information on American troop movements to the British or doing business with known loyalists. Despite his many victories, Benedict Arnold's unpopularity meant that he was often passed over for key commands he badly wanted and felt he deserved. By the time he became the military commander of Philadelphia, Benedict Arnold had a long list of enemies, as well as complaints against the Continental army.

In 1778, Benedict Arnold was a wealthy widower in his late thirties. Peggy was an eighteen-year-old society belle, who probably felt much like her father did about the Revolution. In September, only three months after arriving in the city, General Arnold proposed. At first, Peggy hesitated, and Edward Shippen discouraged the marriage for two reasons. First, the judge probably hoped to prevent an alliance between his youngest child and an American general with a shady reputation. Second, Benedict was twenty years older, as well as lame from a serious leg wound received during the previous winter's attack on Canada.

Later that winter, however, Peggy decided to marry Benedict. When her father balked, she retreated to her room and had "hysterics" until he gave in. The engagement became official in January 1779. From the army camp in February, Benedict Arnold wrote to his fiancée of his affection and his resentment toward the Executive Council of Pennsylvania. On February 9, the council charged him with crimes against the army and published the accusations in the newspaper. Benedict wrote:

"To my Dearest Life: Never did I so ardently long to see or hear from you as at this instant. I am all impatience and anxiety to know how you do. Heavens! What must I have suffered had I continued my journey—the loss of happiness for a few dirty acres. I can almost bless the villainous roads and more villainous men, who oblige me to return. . . . I am heartily tired with my journey, and almost so with human nature. I daily discover so much baseness and ingratitude among mankind that I almost blush at being of the same species, and could quit the stage without regret was it not for some gentle, generous souls like my dear Peggy. . . . Let me beg of you not to suffer the rude attacks on me to give you one moment's uneasiness; they can do me no injury." B. Arnold.[43]

The council accused Benedict Arnold with several wrongdoings and demanded that Congress relieve him of his command of Philadelphia while the charges were examined. Among the charges were treating lesser officers with disrespect, using public wagons for transporting private property, issuing a pass that only the Pennsylvania Council had a right to grant or deny, and showing favor to Tories (loyalists). While the charges were pending, in late March, Benedict Arnold angrily resigned his command of Philadelphia. Congress then dumped the entire matter in the lap of George Washington on April 3.

"Deal with the Lady"

These developments worried Peggy's family, but she herself did not change her mind about the marriage. On April 15, 1779, she became Mrs. Benedict Arnold. Three weeks later, on May 5, General Arnold asked Washington for a military trial so he could publicly deny the charges and clear his name. In June the trial convened and in January 1780, found him guilty of using wagons for his personal use. The other charges were dropped. The punishment was a formal reprimand, which George Washington issued but considered a minor affair. In March 1780, Washington wrote to the Arnolds to congratulate them on the birth of their first child, and to offer Benedict Arnold a place as his number-two general.

In practical terms, General Arnold's punishment had been light, but to him it was just the latest in a series of humiliations that justified his betrayal. He *was* guilty of most of the charges levied against him, as well as other crimes that involved lining his own pockets under the cover of war. Nevertheless, he was bitter, disappointed, and angry. At an earlier date, Washington's offer might have prevented his betrayal. But Washington's offer came too late. A month after Benedict and Peggy married, the two had begun spying for the British.

Peggy Arnold's reasons for spying are murkier than her husband's, for her family destroyed many of her diaries and letters. Peggy may have helped Benedict reluctantly, obediently, willingly, or even enthusiastically. Perhaps her old friend from the days of the British occupation, John André, recruited her. Then she in turn influenced her already disgruntled husband. In truth, no hard evidence proves who influenced whom more. But documents from the British headquarters in New York prove that the duo became full partners in crime. Deal "with the lady," Major André directed the messenger who carried messages across enemy lines. And the messenger did just that.

Angry at the charges levied against him, Benedict Arnold began spying for the British.

Plot to Weaken the Americans

Peggy got in touch with John André, now a major in charge of British intelligence at New York headquarters. Benedict supplied military information, while Peggy encoded, decoded, delivered, and received the letters. In her upstairs bedroom, she created an elaborate code based on numbers and words from the dictionary. Using invisible ink, she wrote down the information. When Major André rinsed the letter with lemon juice or acid, the ink appeared.

From May 1780 to September 1781, the couple provided information on troop movements, supply depot locations, and the number of cannons and arms. They wrote that Washington would leave New Jersey and head north up the Hudson for the summer campaign. The information gave the British general Sir Henry Clinton time to head off the Continental army and strike before it reached its destination. The Arnolds also provided Major André with information that helped the British take Charleston, South Carolina.

After a year of passing along information, the Arnolds grew more ambitious. With André, they hatched an ambitious plot to seriously weaken the Americans by handing the American-held

New York fortress of West Point over to the British. If the British had West Point, they would dominate the critical Hudson-Champlain waterway, which linked New York City to Canada. To set the plot in motion, Benedict Arnold wrote to General Washington in February 1780 and asked for the command of West Point. Washington gave it. For turning West Point over to

The Arnolds provided the British with information about troop movements, supply locations, and the amount of artillery possessed by the Americans.

the British, the Arnolds negotiated a twenty-thousand-pound reward if they succeeded. If they failed, they were promised half that. Not only that, if successful, the socially ambitious Arnolds expected to be made a duke and duchess.

On August 3, Benedict Arnold took command of the fort, and on September 12, Peggy arrived with their infant son. The *Vulture*, a British warship, was anchored twelve miles south on the Hudson River, ready to attack the fort. A few weeks later, Washington announced that he was coming to inspect the troops, and the spy couple saw their opportunity. They planned to capture Washington, then order the *Vulture* to attack the fort. With their commander in chief a prisoner, the Arnolds expected the Americans to surrender.

Peggy feigns hysterics upon learning that her husband has been found out as a spy.

On September 23, the day of Washington's visit, Peggy was upstairs with her son while Benedict Arnold and his staff ate breakfast. A mud-splattered messenger rushed in and announced that Major André had been captured just north of Tarrytown that morning. A group of American soldiers had stopped and stripped André. In his socks they found papers revealing the plot and arrested him.

A Dramatic Scene

Benedict Arnold told his wife that damning evidence against him would soon be in Washington's hands. The papers Major André carried did not reveal Peggy's guilt; she stayed at West Point. Meanwhile, Benedict galloped to the Hudson and jumped into an eighteen-oar barge. He pointed his gun at the American crew and ordered them to row him to the *Vulture*.

As soon as Benedict escaped, his wife turned on hysterics that proved her a fine actress. She pulled pins from her hair and ran screaming through the hall in her nightgown. Servants ran to help her, and she pushed them aside. In letters, officers on the scene wrote of the dramatic scene that followed. When they rushed upstairs, Peggy clutched her baby and cried that her husband was "dead, dead, dead." "Have you ordered my child to be killed?" she wailed repeatedly. Then she fell to her knees and prayed the officers to "spare her innocent babe."[44]

Washington arrived, sent men after Benedict, then questioned the distraught Peggy. When she saw Washington, Peggy wailed: "That is not George Washington. That is the man who was going to assist . . . in killing my child!" Colonel Alexander Hamilton was one of Washington's aides who wrote of Peggy's convincing performance. To his fiancée he wrote:

> Her sufferings were so eloquent that I wished myself her brother to have a right to become her defender. . . . Could I forgive Arnold for sacrificing his honor, reputation, and duty, I could not forgive him for acting a part that must have forfeited the esteem of so fine a woman.[45]

Three days later, on September 26, General Nathanael Green noted the treason in his Orders of the Day. On October 10 his words appeared in the *Pennsylvania Packet*:

> Treason of the blackest dye was yesterday discovered. General Arnold, who is commander at West Point, lost to every sentiment of honor, of public and private obligation, was about to put that important fort into the hands of the enemy. Such an event must have given the American cause a deadly wound if not a fatal stab. Happily, the scheme was timely discovered to prevent the fatal misfortune. The providential train of circumstance which led to it, affords the most convincing proofs that the liberties of America are the object of divine protection. At the same time the treason is so regretted, the General cannot help congratulating the army on the happy discovery. . . . His Excellency the Commander-in-chief has arrived at West Point from Hartford, and is now doubtless taking proper steps to unravel fully so hellish a plot.[46]

"So Delicate and Timorous a Girl"

Like Hamilton, Washington pitied the hysterical young mother. On September 27, he sent her back to her family in Philadelphia. Meanwhile, General Arnold arrived safely in British-held New York and was made a British general. Throughout America, Benedict Arnold instantly became the most hated person alive. On September 30, Peggy Arnold hid in her parents' house while Philadelphians carted an effigy of her husband through the streets. The effigy had two faces—one heroic, one villainous. In one hand

Peggy hid in her parents' mansion while the public vilified her husband with an effigy.

the dummy of Benedict Arnold held a letter from the devil, which said Benedict Arnold must hang himself. Behind him was a dummy of the devil himself, dressed in black robes and holding a pitchfork to drive Benedict Arnold into hell.

Days later, on October 1, 1780, a real hanging took place. John André was tried, found guilty of spying, and hanged. All the hatred that might have been directed at André was redirected toward General Arnold. The public viewed the handsome, young spy as a noble opponent who was just doing his job—and had the misfortune to get caught. Benedict Arnold, however, was a villainous turncoat who got away. A popular broadside about Arnold and André read, in part,

Death of Major Andre

The story came to Arnold, commanding at the Fort:
He called for the Vulture, and sailed for New York;
Now Arnold to New York has gone, a-fighting for his King, And left poor Major Andre on the gallows for to swing.

Andre was executed, he look'd both meek and mild;
Around on the spectators most pleasantly he smiled;
It moved each eye to pity, and every heart there bled,
And everyone wished him releas'd, and Arnold in his stead.[47]

While the public vilified her husband, Peggy Arnold hid in her family's mansion. Privately and publicly, her family declared her innocence. Her father, Edward Shippen, wrote that he was "fully convinced" she had "never participated in the guilt of her perfidious husband." Her brother-in-law, Edward Burd, wrote that "so delicate and timorous a girl as poor Peggy" could not have been involved in "so bold and adventurous a plan. . . . It is impossible she should be engaged in such a wicked one." But memories of Peggy Shippen's association with André and the British during the occupation of Philadelphia had not faded. Pennsylvania officials did not believe that Peggy was the complete innocent she claimed, and some people blamed Peggy Arnold for her husband's downfall. A French major general, the Chevalier de Chastellux, wrote, "It is generally believed, that . . . the charms of this handsome woman contributed not a little to hasten to criminality a mind corrupted by avarice."[48]

On October 27, 1781, Peggy Arnold was ordered to leave the state and join her husband in New York. The Executive Council of Pennsylvania wrote, "Therefore, resolved, that the said Margaret Arnold depart this state within fourteen days from the date hereof, and that she do not return again during the continuance of the present war." Peggy's brother-in-law, Edward Burd, wrote,

> The whole circumstance has involved the family in deepest distress. . . . It makes me melancholy every time I think of the matter. I cannot bear the idea of her re-union. The sacrifice was an immense one at her being married to him at all. It is much more so to be obliged, against her will, to go to the arms of a man who appears to be so very black.[49]

In New York, Peggy Arnold lived next door to British headquarters and gave birth to a second son. Her husband mustered a brigade of American deserters and fought Americans in Virginia. Two months after the British surrendered at Yorktown, on December 15, the Arnolds sailed for England. In return for his spying, General Arnold received a onetime payment of 6,350 pounds. Peggy Arnold and her children fared even better. She was first awarded 500 pounds a year for life. Later that was doubled to 1,000 pounds. Each of Peggy's five children also received 100 pounds a year for life.

Shortly after Peggy's banishment from Philadelphia, a newspaper there declared that Peggy Arnold's actions proved women could be as dangerous as men. It was a mistake to act as if "female opinions are of no consequence in public matters," the editor wrote. "Behold the consequence!"[50]

"I Had Cast My Lot"

With the exception of a few years in Canada, the Arnolds lived in London for the rest of their lives. Unable to get the British army position he wanted, Benedict took to trading again. Like many of the

100,000 exiled loyalists living in England and Canada, Peggy was homesick for America. Yet she was only twenty-one, beautiful, and still socially ambitious. Soon she was a favorite among the London elite. One gentleman declared her "the handsomest woman in England." [51] As she grew older, Peggy's children became her main concern, and her success served them well. The four Arnold boys became British officers, and the daughter married one.

On June 14, 1801, Benedict Arnold died. Three years later, on August 24, 1804, Peggy died of cancer. Shortly before her death, the forty-four-year-old widow wrote to her brother-in-law Edward Burd. The letter hinted at sad secrets she would carry to her grave. "Years of unhappiness have passed," she wrote. "I had cast my lot, complaints were unavailing, and you and my other friends are ignorant of the many causes of uneasiness I have had." [52]

CHAPTER 4

Esther DeBerdt Reed (1746–1780)

In the spring of 1780, the condition and morale of America's soldiers was so dire that General Washington feared mutiny. Dissatisfaction, he wrote, had "worn thin the features of a very dangerous complexion." [53] On May 12, Charleston, South Carolina, had fallen to the British, and conditions grew worse. To ease the soldiers' suffering, native Englishwoman Esther DeBerdt Reed formed the first women's relief organization on American soil. Historian Doris Weatherford writes, "As an Englishwoman who quickly transferred her loyalty to America and who raised significant funds despite the disabilities of pregnancy and disease, Esther Reed should be remembered as a founding mother of the new nation." [54]

Esther's patriotism was evident when she called on American women to take on an active role in the war.

"We Must Be Content"

Esther DeBerdt was born on October 22, 1746, into a prominent family of London traders who did business with many American merchants. The DeBerdts were ardent Whigs. The English Whig Party advocated more power for Parliament, commoners, and American colonists. In contrast, the Tory Party contended that the power to govern belonged to the king and royal family. Little is known about Esther's childhood, except that she received a better-than-average education for the time. Among the things she learned was to admire America—but from a happy distance. There was no place that offered such marvelous opportunities for people of different classes and backgrounds,

Esther felt. But the American colonies lacked the sophistication and culture of her London home.

In 1763, Esther met Joseph Reed when he came to dine at her family's home. The American son of a New Jersey merchant who did business with Esther's father, Joseph was in London studying at a prestigious college of law. Americans could learn law by apprenticing themselves to experienced lawyers, but those who could afford it often studied in London, at the Middle Temple at the Inns of Court. Joseph appreciated Esther's poise and quiet good sense, and Esther admired Joseph's responsible, serious nature. In 1765, they decided to marry. Because Esther did not want to leave her family and homeland, the couple planned to make London their home.

Esther DeBerdt met and married Joseph Reed in London.

When Joseph Reed's father got sick in New Jersey, the couple's plans changed. The Reed family trading firm was in ruins. As the oldest son, Joseph had to rush home to set things right. It took him five years to restore the family business and establish a profitable law firm that would provide for his parents and younger siblings. In London, Esther waited.

In 1769, Joseph finally returned to England to marry Esther DeBerdt. But Esther's father died suddenly, and without a mentor Joseph could not get established in England. The newlyweds had no choice but to marry and return to the colonies. Esther hoped their stay in the American colonies would be temporary. Although she thought Philadelphia a neat, well-planned city, she thought the homes "paltry." To her only brother, still in England, she wrote: "I assure you my dear Dennis, I find this country and England two different places, however, for the present we must be content." [55]

Esther harbored hopes of returning to London for only a few years. By 1774, she knew America was her new, permanent home. She had given birth to three children already, and three more would arrive by 1780. The First Continental Congress was meeting and protesting British "oppression." Also, her husband had firmly established himself as one of the most popular and dynamic lawyers in Philadelphia. Esther wrote to her brother in 1774, saying, "Everything is promising here and there is no prospect for him there." [56]

The Glorious Cause

In April 1775, the Reeds learned of the fighting that took place in Concord and Lexington. Several thousand colonists rallied at Statehouse Square, and Joseph Reed was appointed the second in command of the Philadelphia militia. Before the battles, Esther had still "wished for nothing so much as dependence on the Mother State on proper terms." A month after the fighting, she wrote to her brother: "Civil war, with all its horrors, stains this land. And whatever our fellow-subjects may think, the people here are determined to die or be free." [57]

When the First and Second Continental Congresses met in Philadelphia in 1774 and 1775, Esther became a chief political hostess. No one doubted her loyalty to the patriot cause because she was an Englishwoman. A New York delegate described her as "a most elegant figure" and "a Daughter of Liberty." [58]

In June 1775, an unexpected event took Esther by surprise. Dining at the Reeds' house were Virginia delegates Richard Henry

When the Second Continental Congress convened, Joseph Reed accepted a position as Washington's secretary and was away from home for months.

Lee and Benjamin Harrison, and the newly appointed commander in chief of the Continental army, George Washington. After dinner, the group stayed up all night discussing how best to defend Philadelphia from the British forces. Washington liked the competent Joseph Reed and asked him to ride with him to New York. The party set out in a downpour, guarded by soldiers in peaked leather helmets and high black boots.

Esther expected her husband back within days, but he did not return. Instead he sent a letter saying that he had accepted a position as Washington's secretary and did not know when he'd return home. Esther was surprised—and dismayed. To her brother in England, she wrote:

> An event has taken place which I little thought of, and which I assure you my dear Mr. Reed as little suspected when he went from home . . . his appointment as Secretary to the General. I confess it is a trial I never thought I should have experienced, and therefore am the less prepared to bear it.[59]

Esther's husband would, in fact, be gone for months. His clients were left hanging, and his family suddenly had to exist on a salary "too inconsiderable to be mentioned." But Joseph wrote to his wife that he had felt "bound by every tie of duty and honor to comply with his [Washington's] request."[60] Throughout the war, Joseph Reed held a variety of critical posts and often was at Washington's side. As army secretary and adjutant general it was his job to cope with the grave problems that plagued the "ill-armed and worse clothed"[61] army. With Congress having no power to tax the colonies—and thousands of miles of coastline to defend—it was a difficult task. Gradually, Esther accepted her husband's absence, as she had the notion of a split with Britain. "I cheerfully give up his [Joseph's] profits in business, which were not trifling," she wrote to her brother. "I think the cause in which he is engaged so just, so glorious . . . that private interests and pleasure may and ought to be given up without a murmur."[62]

Mrs. President

From 1776 to 1778, Britain and America fought often near Philadelphia. During that time, when the British neared the city, Esther and her children often left the city to live in remote areas of New Jersey. During those years, Joseph was separated from his family. He traveled with Washington's army and sometimes fought with units of the Pennsylvania militia; only rarely did he visit his family. In 1778, the Pennsylvania Assembly elected Joseph Reed chief executive officer of the Commonwealth of Pennsylvania. After the British ended their occupation of Philadelphia in May 1779, Joseph, Esther, and the children came home.

Like many other refugees, the Reeds found their home had been plundered and damaged. Some fine homes had been used as army stables, with holes cut in parlor floors for manure pits. Reeling from the recent death of her two-year-old daughter, Esther found the city's devastation a cruel blow. The birth of another son brought some comfort, and the Reeds began to reap the benefits of their new political status. The Pennsylvania Assembly called Joseph "Mr. President" and Esther "Mrs. President." The family was housed in a mansion seized from an absent loyalist. Esther wrote to her brother: "We are no longer obliged to leave our houses, or stay there with constant dread and apprehension. These are now past, I hope never to return." [63]

As the war shifted away from Philadelphia, the Reeds' life grew more stable. Yet through her husband, Esther was keenly aware that soldiers were "absolutely perishing for want of clothing" and starving on a diet of "miserable fresh beef, without bread, salt or vegetables." [64] Esther hated Americans who had hobnobbed with the British during the occupation, as well as those who continued to overspend and profit by trading in scarce commodities.

By early 1780, army conditions had not improved. The British continued to win important battles and captured Charleston, South Carolina. And promised military assistance and supplies from the French had not yet arrived. The losses deeply discouraged the Americans, and runaway inflation resulted in common soldiers not being paid or paid in nearly worthless paper money. One battlefield doctor protested the "trash which is tendered to requite [pay] us for our sufferings . . . while in the service of our country." [65] Although she was recovering from smallpox and heavily pregnant with her sixth child, Esther determined to do more than "offer barren wishes for victory." [66]

Sentiments of an American Woman

Reed, now thirty-three years old, knew that the "tender sex" was expected to leave public matters to men. But Esther decided society was wrong. On June 19, 1780, a month after the fall of Charleston, she published a broadside calling on American women to take a more active role in supporting the struggle for independence. Her article, titled "Sentiments of an American Woman," was reprinted in several newspapers throughout July.

Esther discussed—more fully than any American woman had before—the roles and responsibilities of women during wartime. The war had lasted much longer than anyone had expected, she wrote. Soldiers were being neglected and their sacrifices were forgotten. It was time for "the ladies" to pitch in.

In her article, Esther cited the contributions of great heroines of the past to justify her belief that women take a public, if merely supportive, role. She cited as role models Joan of Arc, Helen of Troy, and women who "dug trenches with their feeble hands." [67] American women had a duty to show similar courage, she wrote. Women could give up luxuries, as they had during earlier boycotts, then give the money they saved to the hungry, discouraged American soldiers. "Who amongst us will not renounce with the highest pleasure, those vain ornaments, when she shall consider that the valiant defenders of America will be able to draw some advantage from the money." [68] Women could even "surpass" men in their commitment to the common good, she continued. Such a bold statement was bound to draw criticism—and it did. But the determined Esther wrote that anyone who did not applaud "the women's pure patriotism" [69] was not a good citizen.

Tour of Duty

After "Sentiments" was published in late June, Esther gathered thirty-six wives of Philadelphia's leading patriots. The women, who called themselves the Association, planned a fund-raising campaign to raise money for the army. Hoping to assist the "benevolent scheme," Esther's husband initially asked his commanding officer to approve the fund-raising campaign. On June 20, 1780, Joseph Reed wrote to George Washington:

> The ladies have caught the happy contagion, and in a few days Mrs. Reed will have the honor of writing to you on the subject. It is expected she will have a sum equal to 100,000 pounds to be laid out according to your Excellency's direction in such a way as may be thought most honorable and gratifying to the brave old soldiers who have borne so great a share of the burden of this war. [70]

Washington approved of the plan, and Esther, the treasuress general, called the members together and launched the fund-raising drive. The women divided the city of twenty-four thousand residents into territories and went door to door asking for donations to help the Continental soldiers. Mary Morris came home after the first day of fund-raising and proudly wrote to a friend: "Yesterday we began our tour of duty and had the satisfaction of being very successful."[71] Another participant later wrote to a friend that the women had "consecrated every moment we could spare from our domestic concerns, to the public . . . we have made it a serious business."[72]

The fund-raisers, a determined group, took their project very seriously. They didn't let anyone off the hook, rich or poor, patriot or loyalist. The patriot women were still hostile toward women who had been friendly with the British during the occupation of Philadelphia. The campaign, one fund-raiser noted in a letter, gave such women "an opportunity of relinquishing former errors and of avowing a change of sentiments by their contributions to the general cause of liberty and their country."[73]

Donations were both large and small. The wife of the Marquis de Lafayette—the French general closely allied with the Americans—gave one hundred guineas, the single largest contribution. Tavern maids at the "meanest" alehouses contributed small amounts. Contributors who preferred to remain anonymous were identified as Miss Who You Please, Miss Nobody, Miss Somebody, Miss Humanity, and A Good Whig. Wealthy and middle-class women who claimed they could not afford to make a donation were bluntly advised to go without hairdressers, jewels, and ball gowns—then donate the money they saved. Some who caved in and gave only small amounts were awarded nicknames such as Mrs. Worthlittle and Mrs. Pinching.

Some Philadelphians thought the women's behavior very unladylike. One Philadelphia woman wrote in her diary: "Of all the absurdities, the ladies going about for money exceeded everything; they were so extremely importunate that people were obliged to give them something to get rid of them."[74] A man who refused to donate told of being threatened with having his name published on a list of unpatriotic citizens.

Fund-raisers

Others, however, praised the campaign. Fund-raiser Julia Rush's husband, Congressman Benjamin Rush, proudly wrote to a friend that his wife had become bolder, but also had been pressing him to take more radical positions:

> My dear wife, who you know in the beginning of the war had all the timidity of her sex as to the issue of war and the fate of her husband . . . distinguished herself by her zeal and address in this business, and is now so thoroughly

51

enlisted in the cause of her country that she reproaches me with lukewarmness.[75]

Historian Lyman Butterfield notes that the organization was "the earliest instance of what was to become a familiar American phenomenon . . . the grandmother of the Soldiers' Aid Societies of the War Between the States and of the homefront activities of the Red Cross during the two recent World Wars."[76]

The fund-raisers brought in $300,000, a large sum for the time. Women in Maryland, New Jersey, and Rhode Island organized similar campaigns, although on a smaller scale. In July and August, Esther corresponded with Washington about what should be done with the money. Washington told Esther of the shortage of uniform shirts. "The Soldiery are exceedingly in want of them, and the public have never, for several years past, been able to procure a sufficient quantity to make them comfortable," he wrote. Esther, however, had a different plan. She and the other women felt strongly that the soldiers needed cash:

> An idea prevails among the ladies that the soldiers will not be so much gratified by bestowing an article to which they are entitled from the public, as in some other method with which will convey more fully the idea of a reward for past services and an incitement to future duty. Those who are of this opinion propose the whole of the money to be changed into hard dollars, and giving each soldier two, to be entirely at his own disposal.[77]

Washington responded, firmly, that he wanted new uniform shirts, which the women could sew themselves. The men, Washington said, would merely spend the cash on rum:

> A few provident Soldiers will, probably, avail themselves of the advantages which may result from the generous bounty of two dollars in Specie, but it is equally probable that it will be the means of bringing punishment on a number of others whose inclination to drink overcoming all other considerations too frequently leads them into irregularities and disorders which must be corrected.[78]

In August, a resigned Esther wrote to her husband that she would "endeavor to get the Shirts made as soon as possible."[79]

Mary Beth Norton writes, "Ironically and symbolically, the Philadelphia women of 1780, who had tried to chart an independent course for themselves and to establish an unprecedented nationwide female organization, ended up as what one amused historian had termed 'General Washington's Sewing Circle.'" [80] Yet because the sewing circle was for a political cause, the women of the Association broke new ground for American women. Historian Linda Kerber explains,

> Many historians of women of the Revolution have admired the Philadelphia project excessively. "A noble Example" cried Ezra Stiles. Benjamin Rush, whose wife was an enthusiastic participant in the campaign wrote, "The women of America have at last become principals in the glorious American controversy." But they were not principals, of course, they were fundraisers, and only for a brief time and in a single city. . . . Yet we ought to hesitate before dismissing this effort as short-lived philanthropy. Broadsides that accompanied the drives provided an ideological justification for women's intrusion into politics that would become the standard models throughout the years of the early Republic. [81]

After buying linen, the Association gathered and began sewing twenty-two hundred uniform shirts. On each shirt was the name of the woman who made it. In September, Esther wrote to tell her husband of the group's progress. But before he could answer her letter, Esther contracted a deadly case of dysentery. Crowded, unsanitary army camps bred the deadly disease, spreading it as the soldiers marched from camp to camp. Perhaps weakened by childbirth and smallpox, Esther did not survive. On September 18, 1780, she died, leaving a four-month-old baby, four other children under age eight, and a husband who wrote, "I never knew how much I loved her till I lost her forever." [82]

Sarah Franklin Bache, Benjamin Franklin's daughter, saw that the shirts were finished and delivered to George Washington in the fall. "We wish them to be worn with as much pleasure as they were made," [83] Bache wrote. Four months after Esther died, in January 1781, General Washington wrote to the Association women:

Ladies,

The benevolent office which added luster to the qualities that ornamented your deceased friend could not have descended to more zealous or more deserving successors.

The contributions of the association you represent have exceeded what could have been expected, and the spirit

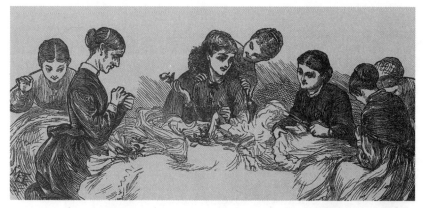

Acting on her conviction that women had a civic duty, Esther Reed organized fund-raisers and formed the Association to make uniform shirts for the men in battle.

that animated the members of it, entitles them to equal place with any who have preceded them in the walk of female patriotism. It embellished the American character with a new trait; by proving that the love of country is blended with those softer domestic virtues, which have always been allowed to be more peculiarly your own.[84]

Opening New Doors

Esther Reed's fund-raising and shirt making was boldly offered, graciously received, and widely praised. Yet, like most women's contributions, it did not change the course of the war in important ways. The impact was long-term, not short-term. Esther founded a trend-setting organization that became a model for other women motivated to contribute to the larger society. Women by the thousands formed and joined charitable organizations to assist the needy: orphans, widows, veterans, slaves, Indians, and others. By acting on her conviction that women had a civic duty to serve the common good, Esther Reed opened new doors for American women.

CHAPTER 5

Deborah Sampson (1760–1827)

In May 1782, Deborah Sampson disguised herself as a man and enlisted in the American army. The war was almost over, but a final peace treaty had not yet been signed and skirmishes were common. Deborah would see enough action to be wounded twice. Around Deborah was a world in turmoil and a nation in the making. She longed to step out of the relatively safe and mundane world of a woman civilian—and into a world of adventure, danger, and honor.

Deborah was not alone. The legendary camp followers, Molly Pitcher (Margaret Corbin) and Captain Molly (Mary Hays), were among the many who helped their wounded husbands on the battlefield. Deborah Sampson, however, is the only woman known to have disguised herself as a man, fought as a soldier in the Revolution, and received an official army pension.

After the war, in 1797, a printer and editorial writer for the *Village Register* in Dedham, Massachusetts, heard of Deborah's exploits. Herman Mann interviewed Deborah about her early life and wartime experiences and wrote a book called *The Female Review: Memoirs of an American Young Lady*. With dramatic flair, Mann retold—and dressed up—Deborah's story. Later, other historians and biographers tracked Deborah's past and wrote more accurate accounts.

Deborah was born the fourth of eight children on December 17, 1760. Her family, New England small farmers, lived in the village of

Disguised as a man, Deborah Sampson was wounded twice in battle.

Plympton, Massachusetts. Some of Deborah's ancestors had been leaders in the colony. Her maternal great-grandfather, William Bradford, had been the second governor of the colony. And on her father's side, the family had a coat of arms. At age five Deborah knew the motto inscribed on it by heart: "Disgrace is Worse than Death." [85] Deborah also knew—and was ashamed—that her own father did not live up to the lofty words. Jonathan Sampson, a bitter man, drank heavily, and the family fell into poverty.

Deborah's mother was not alone in her poverty. A majority of white women in eighteenth-century America resided in poor or middling farm households where they had heavy responsibilities. However, in 1765, things got worse. When Deborah was five, her father deserted the family, went to sea, and never returned. Unable to manage the farm and six surviving children alone, Deborah's mother sent her children to live with relatives and to work as indentured servants. At first, Deborah stayed with family members. Then in 1770, at age ten, she became an indentured servant several miles away, near the village of Middlesborough. For eight years, she did domestic chores and farmwork for Benjamin Thomas's family. The farmer had ten boisterous sons, and Deborah was their companion as well as their servant. The Thomases treated her well, even allowing her to attend the village school if her chores were done. How often Deborah attended school is unknown. But she loved to read, especially Shakespeare's plays about traitorous kings and adventure stories by Jonathan Swift. Later, as a young woman, she was considered learned enough to teach school.

"A Prison of Listless Pursuits"

Deborah was fourteen years old in March 1774, when the British closed the port of Boston. New England farmers sent grain and livestock that they could spare to feed the city. In April 1775, the older Thomas boys marched with the town militia to protect the store of arms at Concord, forty miles away. They joined about two thousand minutemen from all over Massachusetts and fought against an equal number of British. Overnight, a rebellion of a few had become an armed revolution supported by many. After the fighting in Concord and Lexington, Massachusetts country roads were crowded refuges. Deborah saw frightened women and children in carts loaded with tattered furniture, fleeing the scene of the fighting. With Mrs. Thomas, Deborah began melting pewter dishes into musket balls and baking biscuits for colonial soldiers.

In 1777, Deborah's term as an indentured servant ended. She had not lost touch with her mother, who wanted her to marry a particular local merchant. Deborah, however, resisted the match. Mann quoted her as saying the man was a "baboon," who was "intoxicated not with love, but with rum." [86] For Deborah to choose to stay single was unusual and daring. Mary Beth Norton writes that it was assumed women would marry, and single women got little respect in the colonial era:

A white spinster's lot was unenviable: single women usually resided as perpetual dependents in the homes of relatives, helping out with housework, nursing, and child care in exchange for room and board. Even when a woman's skills were sufficient to enable her to earn an independent living, her anomalous position in a society in which marriage was almost universal placed her near the bottom of the social scale.[87]

Though bored with the work, Deborah Sampson supported herself with spinning and weaving.

Despite this, Deborah stayed single and earned her own living for four years before enlisting. To support herself, she sometimes taught school in the summers, substituting for male teachers fighting the war. Mostly, however, she traveled from house to house doing families' spinning and weaving. "Poor women whose training was minimal could always find such work," Norton writes, but it was a "difficult, transient existence." [88] Deborah felt that her days "dragged out in a prison of listless pursuits, tasteless enjoyments and seething discontents." [89]

Although women rarely stepped out of traditional roles, war inspired a few to do the unthinkable. Usually it was because of their political convictions. Historian Doris Weatherford writes,

Sampson presumably joined the military at a time that was right for her and for the same reasons that men did: she wanted the opportunity to see something other than her home area, while also earning a living and accumulating pension rights. Preferring this to teaching in the staid environment of small towns, like men, she answered the liberating call of a new nation.[90]

In the winter of 1781, Deborah borrowed a man's suit from the family with whom she was boarding. Then she slipped out after dark to test her disguise. She strolled through familiar streets, visited area taverns, and drank tankards of ale with the male patrons. When people she had known all her life did not recognize her, she felt confident enough to try enlisting in the army. Deborah's first attempt, on December 17, 1781, failed because the recruiting officer's mother recognized her. Deborah tried to pass her behavior off as a joke, but the young man whose suit she had borrowed told his parents to burn the suit. He'd never wear it again, he said. A year later, Deborah's Baptist church also learned of how she walked freely at night, drank ale with men in taverns, and dressed as a man. They responded by accusing her of being immoral and took away her membership.

According to Third Baptist Church records, September 3, 1782,

> Considered the case of Deborah Sampson, a member of this Church, who last Spring was accused of Dressing in man's Clothes and inlisting as a soldier in the army and altho she was not convicted, yet was strongly suspected of being guilty and for sometime before behaved very loose and unchristian like . . . it is the Church's duty to withdraw fellowship until she returns and makes Christian satisfaction.[91]

Despite her failure, Deborah tried again the following spring. In April 1782, at age twenty-two, she sewed herself a coarse man's suit and white ruffled shirt. In May, she bound her chest with linen cloth and tied her long brown hair back in a ponytail. Then she hiked to Worcester, Massachusetts, where no one knew her and successfully enlisted in the Continental army.

On May 23, 1782, Deborah Sampson became a private in the Fourth Massachusetts Regiment. On the articles of enlistment papers, she signed Robert Shurtleff—the name of her brother who had died when she was eight. Her term was for three years, but she served only eighteen months before being discovered. The army was glad to have all the new recruits it could get, even though the war was almost over. Seven months earlier, on October 19, 1781, the British general Cornwallis had surrendered several thousand troops in Yorktown, Virginia. But a final peace would not be negotiated for two years, and a standing army was still needed. Also, some loyalists and their Indian allies were not admitting defeat, so bloody skirmishes were still common. Deborah would see action enough to be seriously wounded twice.

Deborah was assigned to West Point in New York. The largest of several critical forts north of New York City, it perched on high cliffs above the deep Hudson River. After she arrived, Deborah was assigned to the light infantry of the Fourth Massachusetts Regiment of the army. This was a special honor, for during the height of the war the light infantry had taken on the most difficult assignments. It marched before the main army and began the battle. Sometimes light infantrymen fought with unloaded French muskets, using the attached bayonet only.

The army issued Deborah a deep blue uniform with bone buttons, wrist cuffs, and tight-fitting white pants. On her head she wore a hard leather helmet crested with a strip of bear fur and a long red and black feather. Her hair was cut below her shoulders and swept back in a single ponytail—like the other male soldiers. Like them, she powdered it daily with flour. Deborah learned to drill in formation, load her musket two times a minute, and charge with her bayonet.

About ten thousand soldiers, four hundred women camp followers, and three hundred children shared the hilltop fort. Some of the

Deborah Sampson made herself a man's suit with a ruffled shirt, tied her hair in a ponytail, and enlisted in the Continental army.

women and children were soldiers' family members. Others were refugees. They worked for half wages—as cooks, water carriers, nurses, and washerwomen. Neither the men nor women ever suspected that Robert Shurtleff was really a woman. It wasn't difficult for Deborah to disguise her sex. Although she shared a straw mattress with another soldier at night, everyone slept in their clothes and rarely bathed. Historian Sally Smith Booth explains:

> Deborah was about five feet eight inches tall, not an unusual height in an era when most men six feet tall were considered near giants. Army shirts of the day were loose fitting and by binding her breasts, Deborah evidently managed to appear not significantly different from her fellow soldiers. The lack of a beard was not an obstacle, for the desperate continentals were enlisting teenage youth into the ranks.[92]

"A Brave Young Woman"

Deborah must have stood out as an exceptional soldier, for only weeks after arriving at West Point she was assigned to a special unit of soldiers called rangers. The rangers kept tabs and reported activity on the outskirts of British-held areas. Half of New York was loyalist, and gangs of diehards continued to attack, raid, and burn homes of those who had sided with the Americans. The rangers also pursued and clashed with these brigades.

Deborah's first assignment was in June 1782. Her unit traveled south to Harlem, just eight miles north of British-held New York City. Soon after the unit crossed White Plains fields—where bloody battles had taken place in 1776—it was ambushed. The two sides traded fire and Deborah barely escaped being wounded or killed. In Mann's colorful version of Deborah's adventures, a musket ball tore through her hat, and the feather fell at her feet. The loyalists fled when reinforcements arrived. Among the newcomers was a neighbor of Deborah's from Middlesborough. He did not recognize the sweaty, blood-smeared soldier as Deborah Sampson, itinerant weaver.

A few weeks later, Deborah was with her unit, patrolling the area near Tarrytown. Again a group of loyalists ambushed her patrol. From behind trees, they appeared and began shooting and charging with their bayonets. Although taken by surprise, Deborah was able to fire her musket at the enemy before being slashed in the forehead with a saber and shot in the upper thigh. As her comrades fought on, Deborah's sergeant whisked her onto his horse and fled into the woods. Holding her limp and blood-covered body before him on the saddle, the officer galloped off to a French field hospital a mile or so away. Once there, while the doctor was busy with other patients, Deborah grabbed a silver probe and twisted the inch-deep musket ball out of her thigh. After secretly bandaging herself and resting, she returned to duty. Her leg, however, caused her pain for the rest of her life.

Sometime in October, West Point troops moved to winter headquarters in Windsor, New York. Deborah joined about ten thousand men from New England and the Northeast. It was a wicked winter, and with no more battles to fight, men were restless. Many wanted to go home, but the army would not release them until their terms of service were up. In addition, many had not been paid. Protest letters circulated among the soldiers that winter. The government "tramples on your rights, disdains your cries and insults your distresses,"[93] they declared. Washington sympathized with the soldiers' situation, but he feared mutiny and raids on Congress. Troops were sent to Philadelphia to keep the peace, and in the spring of 1783 Deborah's unit joined them.

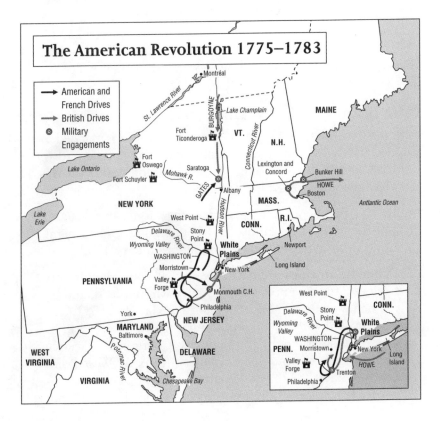

By September 1783, most loyalists and Indians had thrown in the towel, and peace negotiations in Paris were progressing well. It seemed likely that Deborah would see no more fighting and finish her army career without being discovered. But an epidemic of malignant fever swept through the camp in Philadelphia. Deborah caught it and was taken to the Pennsylvania Hospital. There, a doctor discovered Deborah's secret when he examined her. Dr. Binney quickly moved her to his home to recover and apparently did not tell anyone that Private Robert Shurtleff was a woman for more than a month. Deborah continued to dress in men's clothing and pass as a soldier while convalescing. When Deborah felt well enough to return to her unit, the doctor finally asked and received her real name. According to Mann's account, the doctor then said, "You are a brave young woman, Deborah Sampson. Your name will go down in history." [94]

In a letter, Dr. Binney revealed Deborah's true identity to the commander of West Point, General Paterson. After calling Deborah into his office, the general reportedly said, "Private Robert Shurtleff, you have . . . always been brave, vigilant and faithful. . . . Now I must ask you a vital question. Does that uniform conceal a woman's form?" [95] Deborah admitted the truth, and was treated kindly by the astonished general. On October 25, 1783, General Henry Knox—later the first secretary of war—honorably discharged Deborah. Six weeks earlier, a final peace treaty had been signed in Paris.

"The Justness of Her Claim"

Deborah returned to Massachusetts and in 1785 married Benjamin Gannett, who owned a small farm. The couple had three children. In 1792, she petitioned the Commonwealth of Massachusetts for money owed her as a soldier:

> To His Excellency the Governor, the Honorable Senate, and the Honorable House of Representation, in General Court assembled, this Eleventh day of January 1792.
>
> Deborah Gannett Humble Sheweth that your Memorialist from zeal for the good of her country was unduc'd, and by the name of Robert Shurtleff did, on May 20, 1782, . . . was engag'd with the Enemy at Tarry Town, New York, & was wounded there by the enemy & Continued in Service until discharged, by General Henry Knox at West Point October 25, 1783. Your Memorialist has made some Application to receive pay for her services in the Army, but

Deborah presents George Washington with a letter. She petitioned for money owed her as a soldier and received thirty-four pounds a month.

being Female, & not knowing the proper steps to take to get pay for her services, has hitherto not received one farthing for her services . . . your Memorialist prays this Honorable Court to consider the Justness of her Claim, & grant her pay as a good soldier, and your Memorialist as in Duty bound shall ever pray.[96]

The Massachusetts House of Representatives appointed a committee that reviewed Deborah's petition. Officers she served under testified under oath that she had served with honor, but no decision was made until fall 1804. In February of the same year, Boston silversmith Paul Revere wrote a letter that probably turned the tide and at last won Deborah her pension. Revere, who had met Deborah and was moved by her family's poverty, wrote on her behalf:

Sir, . . . We commonly form our idea of the person whom we hear spoken of, whom we have never seen, according as their actions are described. When I heard her spoken of as a soldier, I formed the idea of a tall, masculine female, who had a small share of understanding, without education, and one of the meanest of her sex.—when I saw and discoursed with her I was agreeable surprised to find a small, effeminate, and conversable woman, whose education entitled her to a better situation in life. I have no doubt your humanity will prompt you to do all in your power to afford her some relief. I think her case much more deserving than hundreds to whom Congress has been generous.[97]

The House Committee awarded Deborah a grant of thirty-four pounds and the federal government added $4 a month. The official House response shows that Deborah forced society to admit that women could be brave and heroic *and* virtuous and "honorable."

The said Deborah exhibited an extraordinary instance of female heroism by discharging the duties of a faithful, gallant soldier, and at the same time preserving the virtue & chastity of her sex unsuspected & unblemished, & was discharged from the service with a fair & honorable character.[98]

In 1797, while her petition was being reviewed, Deborah told her story to Herman Mann. That led to an opportunity that helped her add to the family's small income. In 1802 and 1803, Deborah lectured to packed theaters about her war experiences. For her finale, Deborah dressed in her old army uniform and marched about the stage and fired her musket. About the lecture—probably cowritten by Herman Mann—one observer wrote: "She almost made the gun talk." Like many unconventional women of the era, she both apologized for and tried to justify her "unwomanly" behavior. The war, she told her audiences, made her do it:

My achievements are a breach in the decorum of my sex, unquestionable. . . . I must frankly confess I recollect them with a kind of satisfaction. . . .

Know then that my juvenile mind early became inquisitive to understand why . . . a nation separated from us by an ocean more than three thousand miles in extent, should endeavor to enforce on us plans of subjugation. . . . I only seemed to want the license to become one of the severest avengers of wrong. . . . Wrought upon at length, you may say, by an enthusiasm and phrenzy that could brook no control—I burst the tyrant bonds, which held my sex in awe, and clandestinely, or by stealth, grasped an opportunity, which custom and the world seemed to deny, as a natural privilege. And whilst poverty, hunger, nakedness, cold and disease had dwindled the American Armies to a handful—whilst terror and dismay ran through the camps . . . did I throw off the soft bailment of my sex, and assume those of the warrior, already prepared for battle.[99]

In 1818, Deborah petitioned Congress for, and received, a larger federal pension of $8 a month. Nine years later, on April 29, 1827, Deborah contracted an unknown illness and died. A decade later, the government awarded her husband a widower's pension. John Quincy Adams, the son of Abigail and John, introduced the request. The committee wrote,

The whole of the American Revolution records no case like this, and furnishes no other similar example of female heroism, fidelity, and courage. . . . He, indeed, was honored much by being the husband of such a wife.[100]

CHAPTER 6

Mercy Otis Warren (1728–1814)

"Seldom has one woman in any age, acquired such an ascendancy over the strongest by the mere force of powerful intellect, and her influence continued to the close of her life." In the 1850s, writer Elizabeth Ellet wrote these words about playwright Mercy Warren. Ellet collected wartime recollections of elderly people and their children, then compiled them into a book. Of the women she profiled, Ellet thought Mercy Warren was "the most remarkable woman who lived in the days of the American Revolution." [101]

Mercy Warren wrote a history of the Revolution, the first book-length work of serious nonfiction written by an American woman.

Like Abigail Adams, Mercy was a prolific and talented observer who wrote about political events that transformed America. But unlike Abigail Adams, she wrote for publication and with a purpose— furthering her cause. In 1772, Mercy's first anti-British play, *The Adulator*, appeared in a Boston newspaper. Like all her wartime plays, it was published anonymously. After the war, however, Mercy wrote a history of the American Revolution. On that book—the first history book by an American woman—her name was printed for the world to see.

Elegance Devoid of Show

Mercy Otis was born on September 25, 1728, in the village of Barnstable on Cape Cod. She was the third of thirteen children born to James and Mary Otis. On both sides, her parents descended from long lines of successful New England planters and officials. For generations, they had built wealth and power in the colonial government. James Otis, Mercy's father, was a planter, court justice, and speaker of the Massachusetts Assembly. More than once he sought an important royally appointed position that went to Thomas Hutchinson, the royal governor of Massachusetts, or one of his relatives. The Hutchinson and Otis families were bitter rivals before the war; when the Revolution began, they became sworn enemies. In many of Mercy's anti-British plays, Hutchinson was the arch villain. As more Massachusetts residents turned against him, Hutchinson wrote in the front of his family Bible: "I have nourished children and brought them up, and even they have revolted from me." [102]

Mercy's father was not only intensely political but a great thinker and reader. Education was valued so much in the Otis family that James Otis Sr. did something highly unusual for the time: Mercy wanted to be tutored alongside her brothers, and he allowed it. With her brothers, she studied history, philosophy, literature, and religion. Mercy was exposed to many books that fostered her intellectual development and writing skills. In her reading, philosopher John Locke introduced her to the idea that a majority of citizens could run a government instead of kings or an elite group. Sir Walter Raleigh's *History of the World* introduced her to Greek and Roman democracies. In addition, numerous playwrights and poets provided models she could emulate when writing her own poetry and plays. Mercy's exposure to a formal education was so unusual for a woman that she was able to escape the narrow domestic circle in which most women spent their lives. Mercy's superior education also gave her the skills and confidence she needed to contribute in the larger world.

An Encouraging Husband

As a young woman, Mercy's advanced learning showed, and her intelligence commanded respect. Yet despite being elegant and attractive, she remained unmarried at age twenty-five. In an age when most women married in their teens or early twenties, Mercy was considered an "old maid." In general, "clever" women were said to have "masculine" minds, and that was not considered attractive. But one man did not agree with such commonly held notions. James Warren, a Harvard classmate of her favorite brother, James Otis, was drawn to Mercy's "Masculine Genius" *and* the "exquisite delicacy and softness of her Sex." [103] In 1754, when Mercy was twenty-six, she married James Warren. The couple moved to neighboring Plymouth, where they spent the rest of their lives. From 1757 to 1766, the couple had five sons, and Mercy wrote poetry.

Like her father, Mercy's husband had unusually progressive ideas about women. Throughout their life together, he encouraged and promoted his wife's writing. In 1769, when a personal tragedy thrust Mercy into the political arena where women rarely stepped, James supported his wife completely. At age forty-one, Mercy stopped writing poetry about nature and religion—and turned her pen to politics.

Throughout the 1760s, Mercy had admired her brother James, a lawyer and politician. As long as her brother was the shining star in the war of words against Parliament and the king, she was content to watch. In 1761, James Otis had argued in court against the British "Writs of Assistance." The writs had let the British search colonists' ships, homes, and businesses without warrants. Before royally appointed justices in long white wigs, James Otis had argued brilliantly for four hours. He had spoken about the rights of common men to life, liberty, and property and of limiting royal power. A packed courtroom had gasped in unison when James said that abuses of kingly power had cost one monarch his head—and another his throne. Few had ever heard such treasonous words uttered. Some observers were shocked or outraged; others were thrilled. One man who heard Otis argue in court said he had "unleashed ideas" that would "shake this province to its foundation." [104]

"My Dear Brother"

From her Plymouth home near the sea, Mercy had followed her brother's career with pride. The royal dozen who ran Massachusetts had called James Otis a "traitor." James had called them a "dirty, drinking, drabbing, contaminated knot of thieves, beggars and transports." [105] The royalists had called him "Esquire Bluster." James had called them "a parcel of button-makers, pin-makers, horse jockeys, gamesters, pensioners, pimps and whoremasters." [106]

But behind the hotheaded James's brilliance was a troubled man headed for an emotional breakdown. His friend John Adams said James overflowed with energy and brilliance one day but rambled like "a ship without an helm" [107] the next. As the years passed, he grew more troubled. He roamed the city late into the night and harassed friends and enemies alike. By 1769, the magnetic leader of an infant rebel movement was unstable. "Otis talks all," wrote Adams, "he grows the most talkative man alive; no other gentleman in company can find a space to put in words. . . . There is much sense, knowledge, spirit, and humor in his conversation, but he grows narrative, like an old man; abounds in stories."[108] After an ongoing battle of words, James picked a fight with a group of loyalists in a tavern. In the brawl that followed, he was severely beaten and never fully recovered. Soon after the fight, Mercy wrote to her brother:

My dear Brother:

You know not what I have suffered for you within the last 24 hours. . . . I wish to know every circumstance of this guilty affair: Is it possible that we have men among us under the guise of officers of the Crown, who have become open assassins? Have they with a band of ruffians at their heels attacked a gentleman alone and unarmed . . .? Thousands are thanking you . . . and daily praying for the preservation of your life.[109]

James Otis argued against the British practice of searching colonists' belongings without a warrant.

After the fight, James's mental state deteriorated. Two years later, in 1771, Governor Hutchinson wrote in his diary: "Otis was carried off today in a post-chaise, bound hand and foot. He has . . . set the Province in a flame and perished in the attempt."[110]

Fanning the Flames

James Otis's mental collapse probably would have occurred with or without the beating. But Mercy did not believe that. Instead, she blamed the British for her brother's disability. In her eyes, James was a fallen hero, a martyr who sacrificed his sanity for the cause of liberty. If the British won, her brother's sacrifice would be in vain. Mercy seems to have decided that if her brother were not there to fan the flames of the fire, she would do it for him. Not long after his death, she began writing plays that made the British look like fools and tyrants. James had stirred people up with speeches laced with satire and passion. Mercy did the same with her piercing pen.

In 1772, *The Adulator* appeared in the *Massachusetts Spy*. Like many plays of the period, it was meant to be read, not performed. Mercy had no real choice but to publish her plays anonymously, writes her biographer Katherine Anthony: "Ladies were not supposed to write for publication and when they overstepped the bounds in this respect, they concealed themselves modestly behind no signature at all or behind a pseudonym."[111]

The play mimicked real life, as did most of Mercy's plays. Everyone who read the play knew that the characters represented real people: James Otis was Brutus, the hero of Upper Servia (the American colonies). Characters representing James Warren, John Adams, and other rebel leaders also had parts. The play's villain, Rapatio was Thomas Hutchinson, the ruler of Blunderland (Britain). Rapatio planned a massacre (the Boston Massacre) to pay the people

Mercy's play The Adulator *mimicked the real-life event of the Boston Massacre, portraying the British as fools and tyrants.*

back for attacking his house. In the end, Brutus does enter—and plunges "daggers sweated in blood" [112] into Rapatio's heart.

Mercy's second play, *The Defeat*, appeared in 1773. It mirrored another real event. Thomas Hutchinson had by then been replaced as governor and returned to England. But his private letters had been stolen and published. In them, Hutchinson called the rebels a weak minority. "Rapatio" again represented Hutchinson, the villain. But Rapatio could not, of course, "kill the ardent love of liberty in free-born sons." [113]

"For the Good of the World"

In 1774, the first rumblings of war shook Mercy's world and distracted her from writing. General Thomas Gage dissolved the colonial government of Massachusetts, where her husband served. The patriots formed an illegal, independent Provincial Congress of Massachusetts and elected James Warren president. James also was appointed paymaster general of the Continental army and major general of the Massachusetts militia. All men between sixteen and sixty were required to belong to the militia. In times of need, colonial officials called them to duty. In contrast, the newly formed Continental army used only volunteers.

Mercy kept a wagon packed and ready for flight. Often, she rode to see her husband at camp and stopped to see her friend Abigail Adams in Braintree. By 1775, she had resumed her writing. *The Group* appeared in Boston newspapers and featured a loyalist clique who betrayed their country by siding with "Blunderland."

The play was so popular that soldiers passed dog-eared copies to one another in camp. Word spread that Mercy was the author, and she began to feel self-doubt. Mercy worried about damaging her reputation as a woman. Historian Linda Kerber writes,

> In the absence of an established tradition of female public political behavior, many women may have found it difficult to explain precisely their actions outside their private circles. Perhaps the formulaic, ritualized apologies with which they prefaced their political comments were their way of acknowledging that they were doing something unusual. [114]

Mercy sought reassurance from her friend John Adams. She asked if he thought it would damage her "female character" to "paint her enemies . . . in the darkest shades." John Adams had helped Mercy get her plays published, and he considered both her and his own wife to be exceptionally intelligent compared with most women. To ease Mercy's worries—and ensure she continued serving their mutual cause—he wrote, "God Almighty has given you powers . . . for the good of the world . . . instead of being a fault to use them, it would be criminal to neglect them."[115]

In *The Group*, Blunderland and Upper Servia again stand for Britain and America. Again, Rapatio represents the villainous Hutchinson. Other characters are Sylla (General Gage) and loyalists named Brigadier Hate-All, Humbug, Sir Spendall, Hector Mushroom, Dupe, Crusty Crowbar, and Simple Sapling. Rapatio writes to his allies from Blunderland:

> He sends a groan across the broad Atlantic,
> And with a phiz of Crocodilian Stamp,
> Can weep, and wreathe, still hoping to deceive.[116]

Like all Mercy's works, the play is long on words—and short on action. The loyalist characters lounge lazily about their headquarters discussing the conflict and the problems it has caused for them individually. Around them hovers "a swarm of court sycophants, hungry harpies, and unprincipled danglers . . . supported by a mighty army and navy from Blunderland, for the laudable purpose of enslaving its best friends." The characters are greedy, jealous, fearful, guilt-ridden, and hateful. Sylla, for example, advises Brigadier Hate-All to ruthlessly attack the patriots:

> 'Tis now the time to try their daring tempers,
> Send out a few, and if they are cut off,
> What are a thousand souls, sent swiftly down
> To Pluto's gloomy shades?[117]

After John Adams read the play, he wrote that Mercy was a writer with "no equal that I know of in this country."[118]

"Trembling Nerves"

In the spring of 1776, the British were forced out of Boston by the patriots. More than a thousand loyalists crowded onto ships and fled with them to New York. The exodus inspired Mercy to write *The Blockheads* in 1776. After barely surviving a siege by soldiers of Upper Servia, panic-stricken Blunderland officers crowded onto boats bound for home. With them were their Tory friends, Meagre, Surly, Bonny, Simply, Jemima, Tabitha, and Dorsa. "Women, children, soldiers, sailors, governors, councillors, flatterers, statesmen and pimps," Mercy wrote with undisguised contempt, "huddled promiscuously either in fishing boats or Royal barks, whichever offered the first means of escape."[119]

In 1777, Mercy began to have more severe migraine headaches and eye trouble. In later years, she dictated her writing; by the time she died she was blind. When her husband was away from home, Mercy missed him greatly. Often in her letters, she asked him to soothe her "trembling nerves" and "restore her spirits" by coming home. When James could not make it, he suggested that his wife write more plays. "I am sure the remedy will succeed and you will feel a laudable pride," [120] he wrote. Still, concern for his wife did cause James to turn down a chance to lead an army and serve in the Continental Congress.

Mercy's "trembling nerves" are not surprising, given her constant worries over her grown sons: In 1778, the British captured her son Winslow; James was wounded in battle, had a leg amputated, and suffered a mental breakdown; and Charles developed tuberculosis and eventually died. In addition, tragedy struck James Otis, Mercy's brother. After being released from the mental institution, he had been cared for by family friends on a remote farm. Although stabilized, he was still subject to mood swings. One day, he was caught outside in a storm and before he could find shelter he was struck by lightning and killed. These personal and health problems quieted Mercy's pen from 1777 to 1778, but she still had one more patriotic play to contribute.

In 1779, *The Motley Assembly: A Farce* took special aim at loyalists who lived luxuriously while others suffered. In Boston, speculators were making a killing trading in scarce food, clothing, and other supplies. James described the situation in a letter to John Adams on June 13, 1779:

> I am still drudging at the Navy Board for a morsel of bread, while others, and among them fellows who would have cleaned my shoes five years ago, have amassed fortunes and are riding in chariots. . . . Were you to be set down here, you could not realize what you see. You would think you were upon enchanted ground in a world turned topsy-turvy.[121]

Fashionable Tory ladies had prominent roles in the play. Mrs. Bubble and her maid Tabitha are snobs who admire the English aristocracy above all else. In the play, two American officers boldly suggest that a group of ladies make two shirts a week for the Continental soldiers. They refuse, ridicule the American officers behind their backs, and wait for the more elegant British to return. A lowly patriot servant dies, then looks "down with an inconceivable degree of pity and contempt on Kings and Emperors." [122]

Mercy biographer Katherine Anthony writes,

Always Warren's fantasy operated on the greatest scarcity of materials. Her personal life was lived out in one unchanging set of scenes. She never traveled; she never went to boarding school. The little world that she saw from horseback extended at most from Boston to Providence. Her experience of nature was limited to a simple strip of sea-coast. . . . She knew no language but her own—perhaps a smattering of Latin but no French or German. Yet out of this scarcity she penetrated and expressed the profundities of nature and envisaged the growth of a nation. Out of this scarcity she made poems, dramas, and history. . . . In another age, in another climate, her literary talent might have shaped her into an ivory tower character. But the age in which she lived forged her into a public literary and political influence.[123]

"Not the Province of Ladies"

After the war, Mercy published two more plays anonymously. Now that the Revolution was over, her themes changed to romantic tragedies with patriotic themes. The characters in *The Ladies of Castile* and the *Sack of Rome* were warriors and their lady loves. When the heroes died for their country, the heroines were brokenhearted, yet proud. Mercy also wrote a book of poems using her own name. The poems focused largely on love of God, family, and the natural world.

Mercy, however, had not lost interest in public affairs and history. Throughout the war, she had corresponded with a number of far-seeing women with intellectual and political interests. Catharine Macaulay, who had shocked English society by writing a history of England, was among them. Inspired by Macaulay, Mercy wrote a three-volume history of the American Revolution titled *The History of the Rise, Progress, and Termination of the American Revolution, Interspersed with Biographical and Moral Observations*. Published in 1805, when Mercy was seventy-seven years old, it was the first history book written by an American woman. This time the author's name was plain to see: Mercy Warren.

Mercy's book showed great insight, for it predicted that America would someday embrace the idea of the natural equality of all sexes, races, and creeds. Mercy also advocated giving more power to individuals and state governments, rather than having a strong centralized government. She and her husband, James, became anti-federalists, the faction that was the forerunner of the Republican Party. In this, the Warrens split from their old friends John and Abigail Adams, who became federalists. The Federalist Party favored a strong centralized government and was the forerunner of the Democratic Party.

When Mercy wrote openly, using her name, she did not receive as much support as she had as an anonymous patriot playwright. Her ideas were controversial, and people were not accustomed to reading such serious works by women. However, Mercy's longtime friend John Adams was more than disinterested; he was angry and critical. Putting friendship aside, Mercy wrote in her book that Adams had betrayed the principles of the Revolution. Rather than attack her on political grounds, however, Adams chose to criticize her for writing at all. To the woman he once called a genius, he wrote, "History is not the Province of Ladies."[124]

Eventually, the Warren and Adams families set aside their differences and resumed a close friendship. In her final years, Mercy continued writing poetry—dictating to her sons and grandchildren as her eyesight failed. She also corresponded with dozens of young women, family members, and daughters of friends. In hundreds of letters, she encouraged women to educate themselves, as well as their daughters. In 1814, in her eighties, she died.

CHAPTER 7

Phillis Wheatley (1753–1784)

In 1761 European slave traders took seven-year-old Phillis Wheatley from her African homeland to be enslaved in America. By 1773, she had published the first book of poems by an African American woman, toured London, and become a minor celebrity in the northern colonies. In 1775, Phillis publicly lent her voice to the patriot cause, praising commander in chief George Washington in a poem.

A majority of Phillis's forty-six published poems were religious and avoided discussions of politics or race. But as she matured—and gained her freedom—she strayed more often from that cautious approach. Increasingly, she made the argument that blacks deserved freedom from whites, just as America deserved freedom from Britain.

Yet it was Phillis's life, more than her words, that left such a profound legacy. That a female slave could write such poetry seriously weakened arguments that blacks and women were intellectually inferior. That influence extended after her death, when abolitionists who struggled to abolish slavery in America cited Phillis Wheatley as an example of the black achievement. Antislavery activists sometimes quoted these words written by Phillis: "In every human breast, God has implanted a principle, which we call love of freedom. It is impatient of oppression, and pants for deliverance."[125]

Understanding Slavery

Phillis Wheatley's exact birth date is unknown but thought to be sometime in 1753. The slavers estimated Phillis's age at seven because she was losing her baby teeth. Of her early childhood in Africa and the ocean crossing to the colonies, Phillis never wrote. It's not surprising that she would want to forget the ship's crowded wooden shelves where she slept, the odor of raw sewage, the diet of rice and water, and the daily deaths from flu, scurvy, smallpox, and dysentery. Given Phillis's youth and the horror of the slave ship, it's also not surprising that she grew so close to the woman who bought her. Susannah Wheatley, fifty-two, was the wife of a successful Boston merchant. On June 1, 1761, Susannah Wheatley bought the sickly looking child who was wrapped in a carpet scrap. Susannah named her new slave after the ship she had arrived on—the *Phillis*.

In the Wheatleys' large brick house on busy King Street, Phillis was dressed and fed well. She also was trained in the duties of a lady's maid and taught to read and write. When Phillis learned English, she would understand that she was a slave—property that could be bought and sold. Eventually, she would ask to be freed and cautiously oppose slavery. But she never expressed anger toward the owners who had brought her into their world of comfort, learning, and faith. In fact, she adopted most of her owners' deeply religious beliefs and attitudes about slavery. "She was conscious of her color," writes literary critic Julian Mason, "but the degree to which she became a New Englander helped moderate this awareness during her formative years." [126]

Cursed Be Canaan

Only 10 percent of American slaves lived in New England. Most were domestic workers or worked in shops. Many were taught the basics of reading and writing, and in general were treated better than plantation slaves in the South. During and after the Revolution, northern antislavery sentiment grew. But when Phillis arrived in 1761, only a handful of people opposed slavery outright.

Although a slave, Phillis Wheatley was taught to read and write. She eventually went on to publish forty-six poems.

The Wheatleys were Christian Congregationalists, who believed that it was God's plan for society to be structured in a hierarchy, with some races at the top and others at the bottom. Like many New Englanders, the Wheatleys also believed that a particular biblical curse justified slavery. The people of Canaan were black, and the curse read: "Cursed be Canaan; a servant of servants shall he be unto his brethren." [127] Yet the Wheatleys also believed anyone who converted to the Christian faith—black, white, native, rich, poor—became equal to *all* other souls in heaven. Phillis's poetry and letters show how deeply she adopted these beliefs.

Between Black and White

Mary and Nathaniel Wheatley—the eighteen-year-old twin children of the Wheatleys—taught Phillis to speak, read, and write English. By the time she was nine, she could do all three nearly perfectly. Then she began to tackle Latin, geography, astronomy, ancient history, and mythology. As the Wheatleys discovered how brilliant Phillis was, they began to treat her differently than their other house slaves. Susannah, especially, became very close to Phillis. A portrait of the slave hung above the Wheatleys' mantle. Susannah Wheatley liked to show it off. "See! Look at my Phillis!" she said to visitors. "Does she not seem as though she would speak to me!"[128]

Phillis was frail and sickly, so a fire warmed her bedroom in cold months. She stayed with Wheatley relatives in the cool countryside during the heat of summer. When the family dined, house slaves waited on Phillis, as they did on other family members. Other house slaves were not considered her equal. In 1757, another family slave got into trouble for sitting next to thirteen-year-old Phillis. "Do but look at the saucy varlet," Susannah Wheatley said. "If he hasn't the impudence to sit upon the same seat with my Phillis!"[129] Yet Phillis was not a daughter. She was a slave who was loved like a daughter—and there was a difference.

With outsiders, Phillis's status changed. When guests dined at the family table, Phillis served them. At homes of other whites, she sat at a small table alone. That way Phillis wouldn't risk offending those who objected to sharing a table with a slave. As Merle Richmond states, Phillis "inhabited a strange, ambiguous twilight zone between black society and white society."[130]

Phillis's first poem, published when she was about thirteen, appeared in the *Newport Mercury* on December 21, 1767. It told the story of two visitors to the Wheatleys' home who had nearly been shipwrecked off the coast of Cape Cod. Susannah liked the poem so much that she put a candle, inkwell, and quill pen by the poet's bedside. That way, if inspiration struck, she could write in the middle of the night. In 1769, Phillis wrote one of the few poems that mentions Africa. It shows how much she shared the Wheatleys' religious views. In "On Being Brought from Africa to America," fifteen-year-old Phillis expressed her thanks for being enslaved and brought to America:

'Twas mercy brought me from my Pagan land,
Taught my benighted soul to understand,
That there's a God, that there's a savior, too,
Once I redemption neither sought nor knew.

Some view our sable race with scornful eye,
"Their color is a diabolic die."
Remember, Christians, Negroes black as Cain,
May be refin'd and join the angelic train.[131]

"First Martyr for the Common Good"

In 1770, British soldiers patrolled Boston's streets; citizens were boycotting British goods; and the Sons of Liberty were meeting to plot their next move. Phillis read the newspaper daily and sympathized with the rebels. In late February, when an eleven-year-old boy was killed during a street protest, Phillis wrote her first political poem: "The Death of Mr. Snider Murder'd by Richardson."

Snider was killed during a street protest on February 23, 1770, a month before the Boston Massacre. Radicals had erected large wooden signs in the shape of a hand and hung them before the shops of loyalist merchants not participating in the boycotts of British goods. The signs were labeled "Importer!" The riot broke out when a group of loyalists were trying to pull one down. A mob formed and began pelting them with rocks. Christopher Snider was bending to pick up a rock when loyalist Ebenezer Richardson fired his gun into the crowd and killed him. The boy's funeral was the largest ever held in the colonies. Two thousand people, including five hundred schoolchildren, attended despite a huge snowstorm. A portion of Phillis's poem read:

In heavens eternal court it was decreed
Thou the first martyr for the common good
Long hid before, a vile infernal here
Prevents Achilles in his mid career
Where'ere this fury darts his Poisonous breath
All are endanger'd to the shafts of death
The generous Sires beheld the fatal wound
Saw their young champion gasping on the ground. . . .

When this young martial genius did appear
The Tory chief no longer could forbear.
Ripe for destruction, see the wretches doom
He waits the curses of the age to come
In vain he fled, by Justice Swiftly chased

With unexpected dismay disgraced
Be Richardson forever banish'd here.[132]

This first political poem of Phillis's was never published, and neither was a poem she wrote a month later in March 1770. "On the Affray in King-Street, on the Evening of the 5th of March" honored rebels who died during the Boston Massacre. John Wheatley, to avoid trouble, may have discouraged publication of these poems. Others of Phillis's early patriot poems disappeared and may have been destroyed, as well.

"No more, America"

In October 1770, Phillis wrote an elegy, a poem that praises the dead. Her fame spread when the poem, published as a broadside and pamphlet, sold well in Boston, Philadelphia, New York, and London. Susannah Wheatley tirelessly promoted Phillis's work by sending it to newspaper editors, book publishers, and influential friends. The poems probably would not have been published at all if Phillis had been without a white benefactor with connections. Although no one knows Susannah Wheatley's motivation, it was probably not a desire for profit. The family was already well heeled and not in need of funds. Instead, the likely motivation was pride in Phillis's accomplishments, as well as a desire to spread the Christian views that Phillis and Susannah Wheatley shared.

The elegy that turned Phillis from a minor local poet into an international celebrity honored a popular minister, George Whitefield. Whitefield was English, but he had often toured America preaching. In America, he also had many friends and supporters, including Susannah Wheatley. Like Susannah, Reverend Whitefield did not oppose slavery. But he argued for a much broader expression of Christian love and charity than was common for the time. True Christians, he preached, loved everyone, regardless of race, sex, or class.

Phillis's poem was titled "On the Death of that celebrated Divine, and eminent Servant of JESUS CHRIST, the late Reverend, and pious GEORGE WHITEFIELD." It paraphrased a Whitefield sermon:

> "Take him, ye wretched, for your only good,
> Take him, ye starving sinners, for your food;
> Ye thirsty, come to this life-giving stream,
> Ye preachers, take him for your joyful theme;
> Take him dear Americans," he said.
> "Be your complaints on his kind bosom laid.

Take him, ye Africans, he longs for you,
Impartial Savior is his title due:
Wash'd in the fountain of redeeming blood,
You shall be sons, and kings and priests of God." [133]

Whitefield was famous, both in England and America. One of his closest allies in America had been Susannah Wheatley. One of his closest allies in England was the English countess of Huntington. Phillis dedicated the poem about Whitefield to the countess, who invited Phillis to come to London and publish a book of her poetry. It would be three years before Phillis took the countess up on her offer. In the meantime, she wrote a poem for England's Lord Dartmouth, secretary of state for the colonies. It was published in June 1771 in the *New York Journal*.

At the time, Dartmouth had been viewed as a friend to the American cause. In the poem, the young poet made her strongest connection between American liberty and black freedom. "Here for the first time," Richmond writes, "is a spark amid the ashes of piety, a spark of independence, of self-awareness." [134]

Phillis wrote an elegy that turned her into an international celebrity. The elegy honored the popular minister George Whitefield (pictured).

TO THE RIGHT HON! WILLIAM EARL OF DARTMOUTH, HIS MAJESTY'S SECRETARY OF STATE FOR NORTH AMERICA

No more, America, in mournful strain
Of wrongs, and grievance unredress'd complain,
No longer shalt thou dread the iron chain,
Which wanton Tyranny with lawless hand
Had made, and with it meant t'enslave the land. . . .

Should you, my lord, while you peruse my song,
Wonder from whence my love of Freedom sprung,
Whence flow these wishes for the common good,
By feeling hearts alone best understood,
In, my young life, by seeming cruel fate

Was snatch'd from Afric's fancy'd happy seat:
What pangs excruciating must molest,
What sorrows labor in my parent's breast?
Steel'd was the soul and by no misery mov'd
That from a father seiz'd his babe belov'd:
Such, such my case. And can I then but pray
Others may never feel tyrannic sway? [135]

In July 1773, Phillis accepted the countess's invitation and sailed for London. Benjamin Franklin visited her lodgings there, and the Lord Mayor gave her a signed edition of John Milton's *Paradise Lost*. Intellectuals active in a growing British antislavery movement sought her out and gave her newfound confidence in her talents. Phillis wrote to a friend of the "civility and kindness" [136] that the English showed her.

While waiting for a scheduled visit with the countess, Phillis prepared her book of poems for publication. But before the visit could take place—after only six weeks in London—she returned to America. Word arrived that her mistress was seriously ill and longed for her return. This was a cruel blow for Phillis, both personally and professionally. The countess could have helped her career tremendously, and Phillis would not be in London to promote her book when it rolled off the presses. Yet Phillis sailed to Boston to nurse her dying mistress. In September, as Phillis arrived back in the colonies, her book began selling well in London. It featured a portrait of the small, slender poet in a white ruffled cap and neck scarf. She sat before a desk, quill pen in hand, ready to write.

For several months, Phillis nursed her mistress, while reviews of her book appeared in London newspapers. Reactions to her poems had much to do with race and attitudes about slavery. One critic wrote insultingly: "The poems written by this young Negro bear no endemic marks of solar fire or spirit . . . most of these people have a turn for imitation, though they have little or none for invention." [137] Another was concerned that "this ingenious young woman is yet a slave." And one antislavery reviewer wrote, "The people of Boston boast themselves chiefly on their principles of liberty. One such act as the purchase of Phillis's freedom would, in our opinion, have done more honor than hanging a thousand trees with ribbons and emblems." [138]

On My Own Footing

The conflicts with Britain continued to grab most of the headlines, but slavery was becoming a hot issue in America, too. In 1774, antislavery measures would be introduced in the First Continental Congress but be defeated by southern delegates. Antislavery sentiment was growing in America and the debate would resurface in the coming years. Probably, the Wheatley family had long felt pressure to free their celebrated slave. But it took lobbying from Phillis's London fans to make it happen. Sometime between mid-September and mid-October, the Wheatleys set her free. On October 18, Phillis wrote to a friend in England: "Since my return to America my Master, has at the desire of my friends in England, given me my freedom . . . I am now upon my own footing and whatever I get by this [the book] is entirely mine."[139]

Her freedom did not change Phillis's life much at first. She continued to live with her former masters. When shipments of her books arrived, she promoted their sale. In January 1774, an advertisement for the book appeared in the *Boston Gazette*:

This Day Published
Adorn'd with an Elegant Engraving of the Author
POEMS
on various subjects—Religious and Moral,
By Phillis Wheatley, a Negro Girl/Sold by Mess'rs. Cox
& Berry
at their Store, in King Street, Boston.[140]

Freedom did, however, inspire Phillis to discuss publicly how she felt about slavery. On February 11, she wrote a letter to Samson Occum, a Native American minister and friend in New London, Connecticut. It was published in several colonial newspapers during March and April 1774.

Rev'd and honor'd Sir,

I late this Day received your obliging kind Epistle, and am greatly satisfied with your Reasons respecting the Negroes, and think highly reasonable what you offer in Vindication of their natural rights: Those that invade them cannot be insensible that the divine Light is chasing away the thick Darkness. . . . In every human breast, God has implanted a principle, which we call love of freedom. It is impatient of oppression, and pants for deliverance. I will assert that the same principle lives in us. God grant Deliverance in his own way and Time, and get him honor upon all those whose Avarice impels them to countenance and help forward the Calamities of their Fellow Creatures.

P O E M S

O N

VARIOUS SUBJECTS,

RELIGIOUS AND MORAL.

B Y

PHILLIS WHEATLEY,

NEGRO SERVANT to Mr. JOHN WHEATLEY, of BOSTON, in NEW ENGLAND.

LONDON:

Printed for A. BELL, Bookfeller, Aldgate; and fold by Meffrs. COX and BERRY, King-Street, BOSTON.

MDCCLXXIII.

Phillis's book of poems was such a huge success in London that her fans lobbied for her freedom from slavery.

This I desire not for their Hurt, but to convince them of strange Absurdity of their conduct whose Words and Actions are so diametrically opposite.[141]

Occum had the letter published in February 1774, and on March 3, Phillis's mistress died. Their relationship had been complex, but one thing was certain. When Susannah Wheatley died, Phillis lost her greatest supporter. Phillis had "panted for deliverance" and wished her mistress would understand the "strange absurdity" of owning a person she had called daughter. Yet she had loved her mistress. Phillis wrote to a friend: "Let us imagine the loss of a parent, sister or brother. The Tenderness of all these was united in her. I was a poor little outcast and a stranger when she took me in. . . . I presently became a sharer in her most tender affections. I was treated by her more like her child than her servant." [142]

"Proceed, Great Chief"

Phillis was free, twenty-one, and a published author just beginning to promote the sale of her book in the colonies. Then the British closed the Port of Boston, and shipments of her books were stuck in London. When the British arrived in April 1774, Phillis, like ten thousand other residents, dropped everything and fled the city. The next year, while with Mary Wheatley Lothrop (now married) in Rhode Island, Phillis wrote a poem praising George Washington. On October 26, 1775, she sent it to him at headquarters. In the poem Phillis refers to America as "Columbia":

To His Excellency General Washington

Celestial choir! Enthron'd in realms of light,
Columbia's scenes of glorious toils I write,
While freedom's cause her anxious breath alarms,
She flashes dreadful in refulgent arms.
See mother earth her offspring's fate bemoan,
And nations gaze at scenes before unknown!
See the bright beams of heavn's revolving light
Involved in sorrows and veil of night!

The goddess comes, she moves divinely fair,
Olive and laurel bind her golden hair:
Wherever shines this native of the skies,
Unnumber'd charms and recent graces rise.

Muse! Bow propitious while my pen relates
How pour her armies through a thousand gates,
As when Eolus heaven's fair face deforms,
Enwrappe'd in tempest and a night of storms;
Astonish'd ocean feels the wild uproar,
The refulgence surges beat the sounding shore;
Or thick as leaves in Autumn's golden reign,
Such, and so many, moves the warrior's train.
In bright array they seek the work of war

Where high unfurle'd the ensign waves in air.
Shall I to Washington their praise recite?
Enough thou know'st them in the fields of fight.
Thee, first in place and honors,—we demand
The grace and glory of the martial band.
Fam'd for their valour, for the virtues more,
Hear every tongue the guardian aid implore!

One century scarce perform'd its destined round,
When Gallic Powers Columbia's fury found;
And so may you, whoever dares disgrace
The land of freedom's heaven-defended race!
Fix'd are the eyes of nations on the scale,
For in their hopes Columbia's arm prevails.
Anon Britannia droops the pensive head,
While round increase the rising hills of dead. . . .

Proceed, great chief, with virtue on their side,
Thy ev'ry action let the goddess guide.
A crown, a mansion, and a throne that shine,
With gold unfading, Washington! Be thine.[143]

Washington was flattered and on February 10, 1776, wrote to
his adjutant general, Joseph Reed, of Phillis's "great poetical genius." [144] Then the commander in chief wrote to Phillis thanking
her for the "elegant lines" and inviting her to visit him at his headquarters in Cambridge. When the British evacuated Boston in
March 1776, Phillis took Washington up on his offer. The ex-slave
returned to Boston and visited privately, for a half hour, with
Washington. Joseph Reed wrote: "I cannot refrain, however, from
noticing the visit of one, who, though a dark child from Africa
and a bondswoman, received the most polite attention of the
Commander-in-Chief, from whom and his officers, she received
marked attention." [145] The poem, with Washington's letter to
Phillis praising her talents, was published in the *Virginia Gazette*
and the *Pennsylvania Magazine* shortly after the visit, in late
March and April.

"A Condition Too Loathsome"

Phillis had returned to Boston alone. She no longer lived with
Wheatley family members, although they probably still provided
some financial support. Boston was almost unrecognizable.
Shelling had shattered the Wheatley mansion, and the Old South
Church's hand-carved pews had been torn out and turned into hog

George Washington invited Phillis Wheatley to visit him and praised the flattering poem she had written about him.

pens. In a ravaged city, Phillis continued writing poems. But the war made getting them published difficult. Then, in early 1778, John Wheatley died, and her life changed drastically. Although a rich man, her former master left the ex-slave who bore his name nothing in his will. Soon after that, Mary Wheatley Lothrop died, as well. Nathaniel, a loyalist, had moved to England. Phillis had been a beloved "daughter," the toast of London, a great general's guest. Now she was free, black, single, and penniless in a war-torn nation. Phillis did what most colonial women did in similar circumstances—she got married.

Phillis first met John Peters in 1774 and thought him a "very clever . . . complaisant and agreeable" [146] man. After marrying him on April 1, 1778, she did not mention him in her letters or poems. Little is known about John except that he was a free, successful black businessman. Before long, Phillis had given birth twice. But both babies were sickly and died as infants. Phillis's biographers have guessed that she might have had tuberculosis or asthma because she had difficulty breathing and seemed to be "wasting away." At first the couple lived well, in a fashionable house. But the economy was in shambles, and by 1780, John Peters had fallen deeply in debt.

From 1778 to her death in 1784, Phillis continued writing poems and made efforts to publish another book. But her poems brought in little cash, and she did not find backers. By the war's end, Phillis's situation was desperate. John Peters was in jail for unpaid debts, and she lived and worked at a boardinghouse in a poor neighborhood. A friend who visited her there wrote that she and her infant son were "reduced to a condition too loathsome to describe." [147]

On December 5, 1784, Phillis and her infant son died of unknown illnesses. Together, they were buried in an unmarked grave that has never been located. John Peters paid his debts by selling Phillis's copy of *Paradise Lost* and faded from view. Merle Richmond writes,

> Sketchy as it is, the preserved record of her final years—the cold neglect, the poverty, the drudgery, the infant deaths, and finally the circumstances of her own death at age thirty-one—is a searing indictment of slavery, of the cruel nexus of the white-black relationship in the evolution of American society. [148]

Phillis, however, had rarely written about herself or her sufferings—and she did not do so at the end. Instead, in her last poem, she celebrated the struggle for American liberation that she had helped to promote. It was a struggle that, against all odds, had been won. Perhaps that victory gave her hope that blacks would also be free someday. Perhaps that hope brought her a measure of peace. Three weeks after her death, "Liberty and Peace" appeared in pamphlet form. It read, in part,

Liberty and Peace

Descending Peace and Power of War confounds;
From every Tongue celestial Peace resounds:
As for the East th' Illustrious King of Day,
With rising Radiance drives the Shades away,
So Freedom comes array'd with Charms divine,
And in her Train Commerce and Plenty shine. [149]

As a writer, Phillis wielded some influence, including lending her voice to the patriot cause. But it was primarily her life that taught valuable lessons—about the abilities of blacks, about the abilities of women, and about the way inequality destroyed lives. In 1834, a new edition of Phillis's book was published by abolitionists, who found Phillis's life and work a source of inspiration. Yet they also saw it as an indictment of white society. At seven years old, Phillis was forcibly taken from her homeland and family, sold into slavery in a foreign land. But native genius, an education, and owners who nurtured her talents and promoted her work helped her become the first black woman to publish a book of poetry in America.

However, Phillis's support system in the white community was weak and temporary—and dependent on her status as a slave. When her mistress died, she hoped to support herself writing poetry. But without her benefactress, she failed. Then after Phillis's husband fell into debt, none of her former white friends surfaced to pull her out of the poverty into which she'd sunk. As long as Phillis had been a grateful dependent slave, she had supporters. As a freed slave, she was on her own entirely—in a world that had no place for a talented, black, female poet.

NOTES

Introduction: Daughters of Liberty

1. Mary Beth Norton, *Liberty's Daughters: The Revolutionary Experience of American Women, 1750–1800.* Boston: Little, Brown, 1980, p. 156.

2. Norton, *Liberty's Daughters*, p. 177.

Chapter 1: The Seeds of Rebellion

3. Quoted in A. J. Langguth, *Patriots: The Men Who Started the American Revolution.* New York: Simon and Schuster, 1988, p. 190.

Chapter 2: Abigail Smith Adams (1744–1818)

4. Elizabeth Evans, *Weathering the Storm: Women of the American Revolution.* New York: Scribner, 1975, p. 5.

5. Quoted in Lyman Butterfield, ed., *The Adams Family Correspondence*, 4 vols. Cambridge, MA: Bellknapp Press of Harvard University Press, 1950, vol. 3, p. 374.

6. Rosemary Keller, *Patriotism and the Female Sex: Abigail Adams and the American Revolution.* New York: Carlson, 1994, p. 187.

7. Quoted in Phyllis Lee Levin, *Abigail Adams: A Biography.* New York: St. Martin's Press, 1987, p. 6.

8. Quoted in Lynne Withey, *Dearest Friend: A Life of Abigail Adams.* New York: Free Press, 1981, p. 3.

9. Quoted in Langguth, *Patriots*, p. 135.

10. Quoted in Philip Davidson, *Propaganda and the American Revolution, 1763–1783.* Chapel Hill: University of North Carolina Press, 1941, p. 223.

11. Quoted in Keller, *Patriotism and the Female Sex*, p. 51.

12. Quoted in L. H. Butterfield, Marc Friedlander, and Mary-Jo Kline, eds., *The Book of Abigail and John: Selected Letters of the Adams Family, 1762–1784.* Cambridge, MA: Harvard University Press, 1975, p. 54.

13. Quoted in Langguth, *Patriots*, p. 189.

14. Quoted in Levin, *Abigail Adams*, p. 37.

15. Quoted in Butterfield et al., *The Book of Abigail and John*, pp. 83, 86.

16. Quoted in Thomas Fleming, *Liberty: The American Revolution*. New York: Viking, 1997, p. 142.

17. Quoted in Butterfield, *The Adams Family Correspondence*, vol. 1, p. 88.

18. Quoted in Butterfield, *The Adams Family Correspondence*, vol. 2, p. 129.

19. Quoted in Keller, *Patriotism and the Female Sex*, p. 81.

20. Quoted in Sally Smith Booth, *The Women of 1776*. New York: Hastings House, 1973, p. 89.

21. Quoted in Booth, *The Women of 1776*, p. 89.

22. Quoted in Keller, *Patriotism and the Female Sex*, p. 87.

23. Quoted in Evans, *Weathering the Storm*, p. 5.

24. Quoted in Butterfield et al., *The Book of Abigail and John*, p. 328.

25. Quoted in Keller, *Patriotism and the Female Sex*, p. 101.

26. Quoted in Butterfield et al., *The Book of Abigail and John*, p. 113.

27. Quoted in Joy Hakim, *From Colonies to Country*. New York: Oxford University Press, 1993, p. 111.

28. Quoted in Keller, *Patriotism and the Female Sex*, p. 135.

29. Quoted in Linda K. Kerber, *Women of the Republic: Intellect and Ideology in Revolutionary America*. Chapel Hill: University of North Carolina Press, 1980, p. 48.

30. Quoted in Butterfield, *The Adams Family Correspondence*, vol. 3, p. 32.

31. Quoted in Butterfield, *The Adams Family Correspondence*, vol. 3, p. 35.

32. Quoted in Joan R. Gunderson, *To Be Useful to the World: Women in Revolutionary America, 1740–1790*. New York: Twayne, 1996, p. 169.

33. Kerber, *Women of the Republic*, p. 11.

Chapter 3: Peggy Shippen Arnold (1760–1802)

34. Quoted in Willard Sterne Randall, "Mrs. Benedict Arnold," *Quarterly Journal of Military History*, vol. 4, 1992, p. 80.

35. Quoted in Randall, "Mrs. Benedict Arnold," p. 80.

36. Quoted in Randall, "Mrs. Benedict Arnold," p. 81.

37. Quoted in Norton, *Liberty's Daughters*, p. 206.

38. Quoted in Booth, *The Women of 1776*, p. 36.

39. Quoted in Lewis Burd Walker, "The Life of Margaret Shippen Arnold," *Pennsylvania Magazine of History and Biography*, vol. 24, no. 4, 1900, p. 415.

40. Quoted in Randall, "Mrs. Benedict Arnold," p. 62.

41. Quoted in *Morristown: A Military Capital of the American Revolution*, National Park Service Historical Handbook Series, no. 7, Washington, DC, 1950, p. 16.

42. Quoted in James Thomas Flexner, *The Traitor and the Spy: Benedict Arnold and John Andre.* Boston: Little, Brown, 1975, pp. 11, 17.

43. Quoted in Walker, "The Life of Margaret Shippen Arnold," *Pennsylvania Magazine of History and Biography*, vol. 25, no. 1, 1901, pp. 38–39.

44. Quoted in Randall, "Mrs. Benedict Arnold," p. 87.

45. Quoted in Walker, "The Life of Margaret Shippen Arnold," *Pennsylvania Magazine of History and Biography*, vol. 25, no. 1, 1901, pp. 148–49.

46. Quoted in Frank Moore, ed., *The Diary of the American Revolution.* New York: Washington Square Press, 1967, p. 445.

47. Quoted in Moore, *The Diary of the American Revolution*, p. 455.

48. Quoted in Flexner, *The Traitor and the Spy*, pp. 378–79, 380.

49. Quoted in Walker, "The Life of Margaret Shippen Arnold," vol. 25, no. 1, p. 160.

50. Quoted in George F. Scheer and Hugh F. Rankin, *Rebels and Redcoats.* New York/Cleveland: World Publishing, 1957, p. 443.

51. Quoted in Flexner, *The Traitor and the Spy*, p. 399.

52. Quoted in Walker, "The Life of Margaret Shippen Arnold," vol. 25, no. 1, p. 177.

Chapter 4: Esther DeBerdt Reed (1746–1780)

53. Quoted in Lyman H. Butterfield, "General Washington's Sewing Circle," *American Heritage*, vol. 2, Summer 1951, p. 7.

54. Doris Weatherford, *American Women's History: An A to Z of People, Organizations, Issues, and Events.* New York: Prentice Hall, 1994, p. 289.

55. Quoted in William Bradford Reed, *The Life of Esther DeBerdt Reed*. 1853. Reprint, New York: Arno Press, 1971, p. 108.

56. Quoted in John Roche, *Joseph Reed: A Moderate in the American Revolution*. New York: Columbia University Press, 1957, p. 30.

57. Quoted in Reed, *The Life of Esther DeBerdt Reed*, pp. 208, 216.

58. Quoted in Roche, *Joseph Reed*, p. 50.

59. Quoted in Roche, *Joseph Reed*, p. 64.

60. Quoted in Roche, *Joseph Reed*, pp. 65, 66.

61. Quoted in Flexner, *The Traitor and the Spy*, p. 200.

62. Quoted in Reed, *The Life of Esther DeBerdt Reed*, p. 230.

63. Quoted in Reed, *The Life of Esther DeBerdt Reed*, p. 297.

64. Quoted in *Morristown*, p. 17.

65. Quoted in *Morristown*, p. 18.

66. Quoted in Marylynn Salmon, *The Limits of Independence, 1760–1800. Young Oxford History of Women in the United States*, vol. 3, New York: Oxford University Press, 1997, p. 73.

67. Quoted in Salmon, *The Limits of Independence*, p. 73.

68. Quoted in Salmon, *The Limits of Independence*, p. 73.

69. Quoted in Salmon, *The Limits of Independence*, p. 73.

70. Quoted in Butterfield, "General Washington's Sewing Circle," p. 8.

71. Quoted in Evans, *Weathering the Storm*, p. 289.

72. Quoted in Norton, *Liberty's Daughters*, p. 188.

73. Quoted in Norton, *Liberty's Daughters*, p. 181.

74. Quoted in Walker, "The Life of Margaret Shippen Arnold," vol. 25, no. 1, p. 398.

75. Quoted in Booth, *The Women of 1776*, p. 266.

76. Butterfield, "General Washington's Sewing Circle," p. 7.

77. Quoted in Walker, "The Life of Margaret Shippen Arnold," vol. 25, no. 1, p. 400.

78. Quoted in Butterfield, "General Washington's Sewing Circle," p. 10.

79. Quoted in Norton, *Liberty's Daughters*, p. 186.

80. Norton, *Liberty's Daughters*, p. 187.

81. Kerber, *Women of the Republic*, p. 109.

82. Quoted in Kerber, *Women of the Republic*, p. 102.

83. Quoted in Butterfield, "General Washington's Sewing Circle," p. 68.

84. Quoted in Butterfield, "General Washington's Sewing Circle," p. 68.

Chapter 5: Deborah Sampson (1760–1827)

85. Quoted in Lucy Freeman and Alma Halbert Bond, *America's First Female Warrior*. New York: Paragon House, 1992, p. 7.

86. Quoted in Evans, *Weathering the Storm*, p. 306.

87. Norton, *Liberty's Daughters*, p. 41.

88. Norton, *Liberty's Daughters*, p. 141.

89. Quoted in Freeman and Bond, *America's First Female Warrior*, p. 90.

90. Weatherford, *American Women's History*, p. 305.

91. Quoted in Freeman and Bond, *America's First Female Warrior*, p. 183.

92. Booth, *The Women of 1776*, p. 267.

93. Quoted in Moore, *The Diary of the American Revolution*, p. 482.

94. Quoted in Freeman and Bond, *America's First Female Warrior*, p. 37.

95. Quoted in Freeman and Bond, *America's First Female Warrior*, p. 154.

96. Quoted in Freeman and Bond, *America's First Female Warrior*, p. 197.

97. Quoted in Freeman and Bond, *America's First Female Warrior*, pp. 200–201.

98. Quoted in Freeman and Bond, *America's First Female Warrior*, p. 198.

99. Quoted in Freeman and Bond, *America's First Female Warrior*, pp. 190–92.

100. Quoted in Booth, *The Women of 1776*, pp. 269–70.

Chapter 6: Mercy Otis Warren (1728–1814)

101. Quoted in Katherine Anthony, *First Lady of the Revolution*. Port Washington, NY: Kennikat Press, 1972, p. 11.

102. Quoted in Langguth, *Patriots*, p. 105.

103. Quoted in Norton, *Liberty's Daughters*, p. 121.

104. Quoted in Langguth, *Patriots*, p. 24.

105. Quoted in Jean Fritz, *Cast for a Revolution: Some American Friends and Enemies*. Boston: Houghton Mifflin, 1972, p. 58.

106. Quoted in Langguth, *Patriots*, p. 100.

107. Quoted in Fritz, *Cast for a Revolution*, p. 85.

108. Quoted in Anthony, *First Lady of the Revolution*, p. 68.

109. Quoted in Jeffrey H. Richards, *Mercy Otis Warren*. New York: Twayne, 1995, p. 85.

110. Quoted in Anthony, *First Lady of the Revolution*, p. 72.

111. Anthony, *First Lady of the Revolution*, p. 115.

112. Quoted in Anthony, *First Lady of the Revolution*, p. 88.

113. Quoted in Anthony, *First Lady of the Revolution*, p. 85.

114. Kerber, *Women of the Republic*, p. 80.

115. Quoted in Anthony, *First Lady of the Revolution*, p. 95.

116. Quoted in Anthony, *First Lady of the Revolution*, p. 92.

117. Quoted in Anthony, *First Lady of the Revolution*, pp. 92, 94.

118. Quoted in Mercy Warren, *The Group*. 1775. Reprint, Ann Arbor, MI: William L. Clements Library, 1953, pp. 2–3.

119. Quoted in Anthony, *First Lady of the Revolution*, p. 94.

120. Quoted in Anthony, *First Lady of the Revolution*, p. 120.

121. Quoted in Anthony, *First Lady of the Revolution*, p. 112.

122. Anthony, *First Lady of the Revolution*, p. 113.

123. Anthony, *First Lady of the Revolution*, pp. 14–16.

124. Quoted in Anthony, *First Lady of the Revolution*, p. 255.

Chapter 7: Phillis Wheatley (1753–1784)

125. Quoted in John C. Shields, ed., *The Collected Works of Phillis Wheatley*. New York: Oxford University Press, 1988, pp. 176–77.

126. Julian D. Mason, *The Poems of Phillis Wheatley*. Chapel Hill: University of North Carolina Press, 1989, p. 14.

127. Quoted in M. A. Richmond, *Bid the Vassal Soar: Interpretive Essays of the Life and Poetry of Phillis Wheatley and George Moses Horton*. Washington, DC: Howard University Press, 1974, p. 19.

128. Quoted in Geneva Cobb Moore, *Metamorphosis: The Shaping of Phillis Wheatley and Her Poetry*. Dissertation, University of Michigan, 1981, p. 35.

129. Quoted in Moore, *Metamorphosis*, p. 4.

130. Richmond, *Bid the Vassal Soar*, p. 20.

131. Quoted in Ronald Hoffman and Peter J. Albert, *Women in the Age of the American Revolution*. Charlottesville: University Press of Virginia, 1989, pp. 355–56.

132. Quoted in Shields, *The Collected Works of Phillis Wheatley*, pp. 136–37.

133. Quoted in Moore, *Metamorphosis*, p. 52.

134. Richmond, *Bid the Vassal Soar*, p. 29.

135. Quoted in Mason, *The Poems of Phillis Wheatley*, p. 83.

136. Quoted in Moore, *Metamorphosis*, p. 66.

137. Quoted in Shields, *The Collected Works of Phillis Wheatley*, p. 267.

138. Quoted in Richmond, *Bid the Vassal Soar*, p. 54.

139. Quoted in Shields, *The Collected Works of Phillis Wheatley*, p. 170.

140. Richmond, *Bid the Vassal Soar*, p. 35.

141. Quoted in Shields, *The Collected Works of Phillis Wheatley*, pp. 176–77.

142. Quoted in Moore, *Metamorphosis*, p. 70.

143. Quoted in Moore, *Metamorphosis*, p. 70.

144. Quoted in Mason, *The Poems of Phillis Wheatley*, p. 164.

145. Quoted in Moore, *Metamorphosis*, p. 72.

146. Quoted in Shields, *The Collected Works of Phillis Wheatley*, p. 172.

147. Quoted in Margaretta Odell, *Memoir and Poems of Phillis Wheatley*. 1838. Reprint, Miami: Mnemosyne, 1988, p. 28.

148. Quoted in Richmond, *Bid the Vassal Soar*, p. 66.

149. Quoted in Richmond, *Bid the Vassal Soar*, p. 50.

"The Adams Family," *Cobblestone*, November 1993. Family history of John, Abigail, and their children.

"American Revolution Tales," *Cobblestone*, September 1983. Entertaining profiles of real and legendary girls and women of the era.

Natalie Bober, *Abigail Adams: Witness to a Revolution*. New York: Atheneum, 1995. A detailed biography of Adams's life.

Sally Smith Booth, *The Women of 1776*. New York: Hastings House, 1973. Fascinating profiles of a dozen women from all walks of life, based on their diaries and letters.

"British Loyalists," *Cobblestone*, August 1987. Overview of life as it was for loyalists.

Linda Grant Depau, *Founding Mothers: Women in America in the Revolutionary Era*. Boston: Houghton Mifflin, 1975. A detailed and insightful look at diverse women's lives and contributions during the war.

Edward F. Dolan, *The American Revolution: How We Fought the War of Independence*. Brookfield, CT: Millbrook Press, 1995. A complete account of the war.

E. F. Ellet, *The Women of the American Revolution*. Philadelphia: G. W. Jacobs, 1900. A dramatic compilation of women's adventures during the war. Out of print and hard to find.

Elizabeth Evans, *Weathering the Storm: Women of the American Revolution*. New York: Scribner, 1975. Excerpts from diaries of diverse Revolutionary War women.

Jean Fritz, *Cast for a Revolution: Some American Friends and Enemies*. Boston: Houghton Mifflin, 1972. The story of movers and shakers in Massachusetts by an award-winning writer of historical nonfiction.

Carol Greene, *Phillis Wheatley: First African-American Poet*. Chicago: Childrens Press, 1995. A detailed biography of Wheatley.

Joy Hakim, *From Colonies to Country*. New York: Oxford University Press, 1993. Probably the liveliest history book about the Revolution. Hakim makes the war come alive and addresses the roles of women, blacks, Indians, and others.

Daniel C. Littlefield, *Revolutionary Citizens: African-Americans: 1776–1804. Young Oxford History of African-Americans*, vol. 1, New York: Oxford University Press, 1997. A comprehensive, well-researched look at an overlooked segment of Revolutionary society.

Robert McHenry, ed., *Famous American Women: A Biographical Dictionary from Colonial Times to Present*. New York: Dover, 1980. Hundreds of important women from all classes, races, and backgrounds are briefly profiled.

Angela Osborn, *Abigail Adams: American Women of Achievement*. New York: Chelsea House, 1989. Adams's life is explored thoroughly in this biography.

Merle Richmond, *Phillis Wheatley*. New York: Chelsea House, 1988. A definitive biography by a writer with in-depth knowledge of Wheatley's life and work.

Marylynn Salmon, *The Limits of Independence: American Women, 1760–1800*. *Young Oxford History of Women in the United States*, vol. 3. New York: Oxford University Press, 1997. A readable encyclopedia-like look at women during and after the war.

Keith C. Wilbur, *The Revolutionary Soldier, 1775–1783*. Connecticut: Globe Pequot Press, 1993. An illustrated look at the uniforms, food, gear, and life of Revolutionary soldiers.

Karen Zeinert, *Those Remarkable Women of the American Revolution*. Brookfield, CT: Millbrook Press, 1996. A fascinating look at dozens of women who contributed in diverse ways to the war.

WORKS CONSULTED

Books

Charles W. Akers, *Abigail Adams: An American Woman.* Boston: Little, Brown, 1980. An insightful biography of Abigail Adams.

Katherine Anthony, *First Lady of the Revolution.* Port Washington, NY: Kennikat Press, 1972. A detailed biography of Mercy Warren.

Carl Berger, *Broadsides and Bayonets: The Propaganda War of the American Revolution.* Philadelphia: University of Pensylvania Press, 1961. A comprehensive book containing letters, diary entries, songs, broadsides, and other telling documents of the era.

L. H. Butterfield, Marc Friedlander, and Mary-Jo Kline, eds., *The Book of Abigail and John: Selected Letters of the Adams Family, 1762–1784.* Cambridge, MA: Harvard University Press, 1975. One of several books of the extensive correspondence of Abigail and John Adams.

Lyman Butterfield, ed., *The Adams Family Correspondence.* 4 vols. Cambridge, MA: Bellknapp Press of Harvard University Press, 1950. Includes letters of both Abigail and John Adams, including those to friends, officials, and family members.

Lester J. Cappon, *Atlas of Early American History: The Revolutionary Era, 1760–1890.* Princeton, NJ: Princeton University Press, 1976. A good overview of the era.

Philip Davidson, *Propaganda and the American Revolution, 1763–1783.* Chapel Hill: University of North Carolina Press, 1941. A collection of letters, broadsides, articles, and more.

Thomas Fleming, *Liberty: The American Revolution.* New York: Viking, 1997. An excellent book that accompanies a Public Broadcasting documentary series of the same name. A comprehensive history of the war is accompanied by short profiles of important people, excerpts from critical documents, and period art.

James Thomas Flexner, *The Traitor and the Spy: Benedict Arnold and John Andre.* Boston: Little, Brown, 1975. Story of the two spies' relationship and spying activity.

Lucy Freeman and Alma Halbert Bond, *America's First Female Warrior.* New York: Paragon House, 1992. A biography of Deborah Sampson based on careful historical research. Dialogue is taken from Herman Mann's embellished early biography of Sampson.

Jack P. Greene and J. R. Pole, eds., *The Blackwell Encyclopedia of the American Revolution.* Cambridge, MA: Basil Blackwell,

1991. Alphabetized information about battles, people, documents, events, and more.

Joan R. Gunderson, *To Be Useful to the World: Women in Revolutionary America, 1740–1790.* New York: Twayne, 1996. This book in the American Women, 1600–1900, series is a current examination of the domestic and public roles of diverse women.

Christopher Hibbert, *Redcoats and Rebels: The American Revolution Through British Eyes.* New York: Avon Books, 1991. A history that shows the perspective of the "other" side.

Ronald Hoffman and Peter J. Albert, *Women in the Age of the American Revolution.* Charlottesville: University Press of Virginia, 1989. Essays by scholars on women's activities, contributions, and roles.

Rosemary Keller, *Patriotism and the Female Sex: Abigail Adams and the American Revolution.* New York: Carlson, 1994. An examination of Abigail Adams's political development.

Linda K. Kerber, *Women of the Republic: Intellect and Ideology in Revolutionary America.* Chapel Hill: University of North Carolina Press, 1980. An examination of women's political development in the colonial era.

A. J. Langguth, *Patriots: The Men Who Started the American Revolution.* New York: Simon and Schuster, 1988. A compelling account of the war through the eyes of key players.

Phyllis Lee Levin, *Abigail Adams: A Biography.* New York: St. Martin's Press, 1987. A detailed account of Adams's life.

Herman Mann, *The Female Review: Life of Deborah Sampson.* 1797. Reprint, New York: Arno Press, 1972. A gripping tale of Sampson's life, filled with battle, shipwreck, pomp, hardship, and intrigue. It's difficult to determine how many of the details were fabricated by the author.

Julian D. Mason, *The Poems of Phillis Wheatley.* Chapel Hill: University of North Carolina Press, 1989. Contains Wheatley's actual writing, as well as insightful analysis.

Frank Moore, ed., *The Diary of the American Revolution.* New York: Washington Square Press, 1967. Letters and diary excerpts that shed light on events and issues of the time.

Geneva Cobb Moore, *Metamorphosis: The Shaping of Phillis Wheatley and Her Poetry.* Dissertation, University of Michigan, 1981. A thoughtful examination of the poet's life and work.

Mary Beth Norton, *Liberty's Daughters: The Revolutionary Experience of American Women, 1750–1800.* Boston: Little, Brown, 1980. An investigation of women's social and political roles.

Margaretta Odell, *Memoir and Poems of Phillis Wheatley*. 1838. Reprint, Miami: Mnemosyne, 1988. A dated biography by a woman distantly related to the Wheatley family. Includes anecdotal information from people who knew Phillis Wheatley.

William Bradford Reed, *The Life of Esther DeBerdt Reed*. 1853. Reprint, New York: Arno Press, 1971. A sympathetic biography by Esther Reed's grandson, which documents her life chronologically.

Jeffrey H. Richards, *Mercy Otis Warren*. New York: Twayne, 1995. A recent scholarly look at the writer's life and work. Very comprehensive and up-to-date.

M. A. Richmond, *Bid the Vassal Soar: Interpretive Essays of the Life and Poetry of Phillis Wheatley and George Moses Horton*. Washington, DC: Howard University Press, 1974. A detailed, comparative analysis of how two early black poets' experiences influenced their literary styles.

John Roche, *Joseph Reed: A Moderate in the American Revolution*. New York: Columbia University Press, 1957. A biography with a political focus.

George F. Scheer and Hugh F. Rankin, *Rebels and Redcoats*. New York/Cleveland: World Publishing, 1957. A lively narrative history of the Revolution.

John C. Shields, ed., *The Collected Works of Phillis Wheatley*. New York: Oxford University Press, 1988. Another compilation of Wheatley's works, as well as literary analysis of her work.

Cynthia Lee Thomas, *Margaret Shippen Arnold: The Life of an Eighteenth-Century Upper-Class American Woman*. M. A. Thesis, University of Houston, Central Campus, Dept. of History, December 1982. Provides details on Peggy Arnold that are hard to find elsewhere.

Harry Stanton Tillotson, *The Exquisite Exile: The Life and Fortunes of Mrs. Benedict Arnold*. Boston: Lothrop, Lee & Shepard, 1932. An account of both Benedict and Peggy Arnold's spying activities.

Carl Van Doren, *Secret History of the American Revolution: An Account of the Conspiracies of Benedict Arnold and Numerous Others*. New York: Viking, 1941. Contains the British headquarters documents that proved Peggy Arnold was a willing and active participant in her husband's activities.

Mercy Warren, *The Group*. 1775. Reprint, Ann Arbor, MI: William L. Clements Library, 1953. Mercy Warren's most popular play.

Doris Weatherford, *American Women's History: An A to Z of People, Organizations, Issues, and Events*. New York: Prentice Hall, 1994. An excellent compilation of entries relating to women's history in America.

Lynne Withey, *Dearest Friend: A Life of Abigail Adams.* New York: Free Press, 1981. Another look at America's first feminist.

Websites

Address: http://history1700s.miningco.com/library/weekly/mpreviss. htm Contains speeches from the era, including a famous one by Mercy Warren's brother James Otis, as well as other letters and documents of the period.

Address: http://lcweb2.loc.gov/ammem/gwhtml/gwhome.html George Washington Papers at the Library of Congress on the American Memory Collections. Includes correspondence, letter books, commonplace books, diaries, journals, financial account books, military records, reports, and notes, accumulated by Washington from 1741 through 1799. Very useful for researching many aspects of the war.

Address: http://www.ushistory.org/valleyforge Virtual Marching Tour of the American Revolution, Valley Forge Historical Society. A comprehensive tour of the war, with links to related websites.

Periodicals

Lyman H. Butterfield, "General Washington's Sewing Circle," *American Heritage*, vol. 2, Summer 1951. An information-packed article about the Association headed by Esther Reed.

J. D. Goodfriend, "The Life of Margaret Shippen Arnold," *Pennsylvania Magazine of History and Biography*, vol. 45, no. 2, 1990, pp. 221–55. Information about Peggy Arnold's postwar life in England.

Willard Sterne Randall, "Mrs. Benedict Arnold," *Quarterly Journal of Military History*, vol. 4, 1992. A current look at Peggy Arnold's life and involvement in spying.

Esther DeBerdt Reed, "The Sentiments of an American Woman," *Pennsylvania Magazine of History and Biography*, vol. 18, 1894. A reprint of the original pamphlet.

Lewis Burd Walker, "The Life of Margaret Shippen," *Pennsylvania Magazine of History and Biography*, vol. 24, no. 4, 1900; vol. 25, no. 1, 1901. An overview of Peggy Arnold's life and a dated account of her involvement with spying.

Other Sources

Independence, Independence National Historical Park, pamphlet 17. Washington, DC: National Park Service, 1956. A Park Service brochure that provides background about Philadelphia.

Morristown: A Military Capital of the American Revolution, National Park Service Historical Handbook Series, no. 7. Washington, DC, 1950. Information about the Continental army's conditions in an area that saw considerable fighting.

Yorktown and the Siege of 1781, National Park Service Historical Handbook Series, no. 14. Washington, DC, 1957. Details the last battle of the war and the British surrender.

INDEX

Adams, Abigail, 8–9
  bond with husband, 29
  Boston Massacre and, 23
  death of, 30
  friendships of, 71, 75
  marriage/children of, 20–21
  reaction to war, 25–26
  on women's rights, 26–27, 28
  youth of, 19–20
Adams, John, 75
  bond with wife, 29
  Boston Massacre and, 22–23
  on James Otis, 68–69
  letters to, 9, 19, 26
  marriage of, 20–21
  on Mercy Warren, 71–72
  as vice president, 30
  on women's rights, 27–28
Adams, John Quincy, 30
Adulator, The (play), 66, 70
André, John, 33
  capture of, 40
  hanging of, 42
  spying by, 34, 38
Anthony, Katherine, 70, 74
army
  establishment of, 25
  fund-raising for, 50–52
  shirt making for, 52–54
  women in, 55, 58–62
Arnold, Benedict, 9, 33
  in exile/death, 44
  military leadership of, 35–36
  spying by, 38–40
    reasons for, 37–38
  unpopularity of, 36–37,
    41–42
Arnold, Peggy Shippen, 8, 9, 18
  in exile/death, 43–44
  after husband's escape, 40–41
  marriage of, 36
  portrayal of, 31

spying by, 38–40
youth of, 31–34
Association, the, 50, 52, 53

Bache, Sarah Franklin, 53
Battle of Bunker Hill, 25
Blockheads, The (play), 72
Booth, Sally Smith, 60
Boston Massacre, 16–17, 22–23
Boston Tea Party, 23
boycotts, 17
Breed's Hill, 25
British
  control of land and, 12–14
  massacre by, 21–22
  occupation by, 33–35
  plays against, 70, 71, 72
  reactions to rebellions by,
    24–25
  taxes and, 14–17
  at war, 18
  see also loyalists
Burd, Edward, 42–43
Burgoyne, John, 25
Butterfield, Lyman, 52

Captain Molly, 55
Chastellux, Chevalier de, 43
Clinton, Sir Henry, 25, 38
colonists
  control of land and, 12–14
  revolts by, 15–17
  at war, 18
Corbin, Margaret, 55

Daughters of Liberty, 15
Declaration of Independence,
  17, 26, 28
Declaratory Act, 16
Defeat, The (play), 71
Democratic Party, 75
demonstrations. *See* revolts

PICTURE CREDITS

Cover photo: North Wind Picture Archives (background photo and bottom left), Archive Photos (top left), *Dictionary of American Portraits* published by Dover Publications, 1967 (top right)

Archive Photos, 45, 59, 63

Dictionary of American Portraits, Dover Publications, Inc., 66, 81

Library of Congress, 16, 19, 21, 77

North Wind Picture Archives, 9, 31, 34, 38, 39, 40, 42, 46, 55, 57, 70, 87

Stock Montage, Inc., 10, 15, 17, 23, 47, 84

The American Revolution, Dover Publications, Inc., 25, 35, 69

Trades and Occupations, Dover Publications, Inc., 29, 54

About the Author

For the past fifteen years, Mary Rodd Furbee has worked as a staff and freelance writer, editor, and television producer. She currently teaches half-time at the West Virginia University School of Journalism and writes adult and children's books, as well as newspaper and magazine features. Her work has appeared in the *Washington Post*, *Stars & Stripes*, *Cleveland Plain Dealer*, *Charleston Gazette*, the *Progressive*, *Goldenseal*, *Now & Then*, and numerous other publications. Furbee is also the author of *The Complete Guide to West Virginia Inns* and *Anne Bailey: Frontier Scout*.

A few years ago, Furbee was working as a lifestyles editor on a daily newspaper. For an upcoming Fourth of July holiday spread, she was fishing for a unique topic and suddenly wondered, what were women up to during the Revolutionary War? The results of her research astounded her—and got her hooked on the subject. America's founding mothers were an enduring, inspirational, history-making group, whose contributions and stories deserved to be remembered and honored. The result was this book.